GOD
KISSES

The Journey Through The Loss Of My Daughter And Finding My Soul

GINGER REYNOLDS

WestBow
PRESS
A DIVISION OF THOMAS NELSON

WestBow Press books may be ordered through booksellers or by contacting:

WestBow Press
A Division of Thomas Nelson
1663 Liberty Drive
Bloomington, IN 47403
www.westbowpress.com
1-(866) 928-1240

ISBN: 978-1-4497-9669-3 (sc)
ISBN: 978-1-4497-9668-6 (hc)
ISBN: 978-1-4497-9670-9 (e)

Library of Congress Control Number: 2013909597

Printed in the United States of America.

WestBow Press rev. date: 07/26/2013

"REVIEWS"

"God Kisses takes the reader on a vivid journey of a mother who is forced to confront the sudden death of her precious daughter. In her beautifully written words, I experienced her full surrender to the devastating pain that loss brought. As the book unfolds, so does her slow growing awareness of God, and deeper appreciation for every day as a day filled with hope. ~Betsy Godbold-Executive Pastor for Care and Spiritual Formations of White's Chapel United Methodist Church of Southlake, Texas~

"God Kisses" is the gripping and painful story of one mother's journey to the brink and back. Surrounded by the silence and emptiness that cripple most after the loss of a child, Reynolds offers a vulnerable story of hope. Through the darkness of grief and doubt, she reminds us of the power of faith and the need to rediscover the true purpose of our lives; to kiss and be kissed by the Almighty. ~Dr. Todd Renner-Teaching Pastor & Provost of White's Chapel United Methodist Church of Southlake, Texas~

"God Kisses" is a must read for any parent dealing with the loss of a child. This book gives insight to the spiritual world from the temporal world through encounters with her heavenly daughter. Ginger Reynolds, through her raw emotions, takes the reader on a journey of proving just how real heaven is and how life continues after death. It is a book that will touch your heart and soul. ~Marsha Maring-Author of "I Know The Secret"~

FOR TAYLER

BECAUSE OF YOU,
I LIVE THROUGH YOUR EYES
BECAUSE OF GOD, I LIVE FOR MY PURPOSE
BECAUSE OF ETERNAL LIFE,
I HAVE HOPE TO SEE YOU ONCE AGAIN

TABLE OF CONTENTS

PREFACE

"God Kisses", this is what I have felt every time God did something extra ordinary for me during this journey. Just like a Father consoling his child that is what God did for me. Losing my daughter at 13 years old has been so devastating and life changing, it's hard to fathom. But God has been with me every step of the way. I didn't see God at first, only anger. But with time and focusing on Him, I started to change, resurrecting into the woman God has created me to be. Oh, I still have a long way to go, but now know with His strength and grace I can survive this.

You will read about my journey throughout this book basically in a time-line format. I truly believe with all of the visitation dreams, visions, and signs you will read about are from God to me. My faith was weak; He gave me these gifts to make my faith stronger. In Corinthians 5:7, "For we walk by faith, not by sight" is how a strong Christian walks. God knowing exactly where I was on my faith journey blessed me with each and every one of these "kisses".

I couldn't read enough at the beginning of this journey wanting answers, "why my daughter?" I read everything from life after death books, Christian books, near death experiences, anything about heaven, angels in our lives, signs and spiritual orbs. I couldn't consume enough on these subjects. But now, my strength comes from the bible and getting to know Christ. I still haven't found "the answer" to our situation, and realize we will never know on this side of the veil. But I have found peace and joy once again.

I pray those who read this book that you find some comfort in my journey and also find God among these pages. If you are suffering the loss of a child, it's something no one else can even imagine the pain we feel. If you are seeking for something greater than life itself, I pray you find God, get to know Him and live life through Him for He truly is the only way.

In John 8:12, "Jesus spoke, "I am the light of the world. Whoever follows me will never walk in darkness but will have the light of life." (NIV) I am not a religious scholar, or have any formal education on this matter; this is strictly what I've learned through my experience, I learned through reading and opening up my heart for the truth. This is my perspective on my experience.

Only through God have I found life again worth living. Yes, I adore my husband and son and am so blessed to still have them, but God gives me that daily love, strength and grace to walk through life. It is through Him I have that promise which gives me hope of eternal life. I will be reunited with my loved ones when my journey is complete. I give all of the glory to God and the Holy Spirit who brought this story to life for this book through me. God Bless you all.

Ginger Reynolds

ACKNOWLEDGEMENTS

First and foremost, thank you to my God, King of all Kings, Lord of all Lords. He is my savior; above all things and I wouldn't be alive and well if not for His grace, mercy, strength and love, to see me through.

My husband Charlie, who is my soul mate and my son Chase, who I adore and love with all of my heart, thank you for loving me and being in my life. Unfortunately we have had to travel this road together, but I am so appreciative for all of the love and support you two have given me. I couldn't have done it without you.

Betsy Godbold, my grief counselor, my pastor, and friend. You are an angel from heaven, and I thank God everyday for you and all of the wonderful insight and help you've given me. I will cherish our friendship forever.

To our church and pastors, John McKellar, Todd Renner, Steven Bell, Jo Ponder, Dara Austin, Judy Hunt and Marilyn Zemba you all inspire me to be the best God loving Christian woman. I am so proud to be a member of White's Chapel United Methodist Church in Southlake, Texas.

My family, mom, dad, step-mom, sister Kathy, all of Charlie's family have been amazing throughout this journey. I love you all tremendously.

I am blessed with so many precious friends but I have to thank Aleda Barry and Susan Simmons for being there for me from day one. You stayed by my side continually, calling, or dropping in on me, just to check on me. I love you both.

Old friends, (Cheryl Raley, Cynthia Jones, Nesa Anders, Laura Gilbert, Sharon Moon), college sorority sisters (Louanne Grimes, Beth Noe, Chris Cox, Kathy Thraillkill, Cindy Stokes, Diane Robinson, Gail Groce, Vanessa McCauley, Pam Bowen, Kathy Johns, and many more) and angels in disguise (Marsha Maring, Rhonda Moorefield, Stephanie Dreiling, Laraine Stevens, and Lynda Langois) were there from sleepovers, lunches, phone calls to just coming to visit with open arms and ears to listen to my endless stories about Tayler and the endless tears that came along with it.

Next are the real angels and "daughters" I am so blessed to have in my life. Tayler's best friends, Nyse Barry, Jess Berry, Lauren Berry, Lauren Earthman, Mallory Kempker, Lindsay First, Mika Ryan, Brooklynne Young, Kelsey Welding, Maddie Wolbert. and Maddie Edson. These girls continue to bless me and I am so thankful God put them in my life.

Last but not least, the wonderful bible study I belong to on Wednesday mornings that consists of the most beautiful Christian women I have ever known. Christie Penn, Marcie Moore, Michelle Stiles, Debbie Page, Deby Garrison, Beverly Lee, Kathy Stephens, Rosemary Kayem, Shari Wellman, Nancy Wagner, Barbara Benson, Joanne Schweitzer, and Shelly Hubel have all personally touched my life and have helped me build my faith even more. They have loved me and supported me unconditionally, and I will forever be grateful.

Chapter 1

"Diseases can be our spiritual flat tires-
disruptions in our lives that seem to
be disasters at the time but end by
redirecting our lives in a meaningful way."
~Bernie S. Siegel~

My daughter Tayler is such a precious soul. She loves life and always seemed to be happy. From the time she could hold a crayon, she was drawing rainbows and butterflies. Nothing but smiles, giggles, and hugs did my daughter live day to day, loving life.

We had a great summer before 8th grade started, taking her best friend Nyse to the Atlantis in the Bahamas. Back home, just the usual, busy with friends, going to the movies, sleepovers, eating out and shopping. Tayler was a social butterfly, always wanting her girlfriends with her. Before long we were shopping for clothes and school supplies getting ready for school to start. Tayler was excited to see her friends again at school.

Everything was going along quite normal until right after Thanksgiving 2008, Tayler started to limp. She said her leg was hurting her and had been for a while. We just thought maybe she hurt it running cross-country for her P.E. class. So I told her to take it easy and I would write her teacher for an excuse not to run for a couple of days. The pain seemed to continue so I made an appointment for an orthopedic Doctor to take a look at it. They took x-rays and his opinion was a possible strain of her "growth plate". He said, "she could possibly fracture her growth plate if she continues to run on it". Tayler was growing taller so instead of risking that ever happening I told her "no more running." So I wrote her teacher explaining the issue and that Tayler could not run in this class anymore. Tayler was thrilled!

Well, we thought that took care of that issue, and went on with life. A couple of weeks go by and still the limping, so back to the doctors and he now puts her in 6 weeks of physical training to strengthen her leg. Sure enough, that didn't help, so I took her to a second doctor and he did an MRI and that's when we saw this dark discoloration on her bone between her knee and ankle. He told us that it possibly could be from a past injury, and said the area that had been bothering actually looked better! He then suggested for us to take her to another doctor, a sports orthopedic doctor for children, and see what he suggests. He may see this and have more experience with child injuries.

So off we go to Dr. #3 and he takes an x-ray and seems to think her leg is healing! Compared to the first x-ray, it had improved. We were leaving for St. Kitts for spring break for a week and the only thing he told her to do was "take it easy." She was going to try out for drill team when we returned so stretching was all he wanted her to do. Whew, that's a relief! Before we had left, Dr. #2 calls back and gives us another Dr. he thinks we need to take Tayler to, "a bone specialist specializing in diseases." What?!? Okay, now I am starting to really worry a lot, this doesn't sound good. Dr. #2 said, "I think this is more than an injury, and I would advise you to see Dr. #4, the bone specialist. Just to ease our mind we go before our trip and Dr. #4 looks at her x-rays and says when we return he wants to do an MRI with contrast. That way we can see for sure what's going on, if anything.

Tayler seems nervous and worried but I am such a positive person, I tell her everything will be fine! She trusts me and believes me, so we fly off to St. Kitts for fun in the sun. After the first couple of days, Tayler was doing okay and seemed to be enjoying herself. We did some sightseeing, shopping and laying by the pool, and really no issue at that point. By the third day, she was in so much pain her knee starts to swell. I call the airlines and can only get Tayler and I out that day back home, so we fly home immediately. We got in to see Dr. #3, the youth athletic orthopedic and he had to drain her knee. I felt so bad for Tayler, to watch her go through this. The next week we see Dr. #4 who does the MRI with contrast and now he says, a bone biopsy would truly tell us what this is! This is now scaring us to death, and Tayler is refusing to have this surgery. Again, we talk her into this, for her own good and so we would know how to "fix" this. The Dr. had a cancellation the next day for the biopsy, so in she goes that next morning.

Bright and early we arrive at the hospital to have this done. To see my baby go through all of this is breaking my heart. What is going on? She is too young for anything like this to be happening to my child! We kiss her good-bye and an hour or so goes by. The Dr. comes out and takes Charlie and I into a private room and tells us it is cancer!!! He tells us he won't know for five days what type it is. We immediately start to cry and Charlie tells him, "what ever it is we want you to refer the best possible place to take her for treatment." When we see Tayler she asks right away, "what is it mommy?" I tell her we don't know yet for sure, and we have to wait until next week when the results come in. You talk about tough, trying to stay calm and happy for the next five days!

The following Tuesday, March 31st, 2009, the Dr. calls us to tell us it's Leukemia, and to take her to Children's Medical Center in Dallas, they are standing by. The nightmare continues, the beginning of what was to come….

Chapter 2

> "Life is like a library owned by the author.
> In it are a few books which he wrote himself,
> but most of them were written for him."
> ~Harry Emerson Fosdick~

I grew up in suburbia, in a middle class family of six. My mother was raised with religion in her life and my father was an atheist. I didn't know what that meant; I just knew God was not brought up in our house. We never said a prayer before our meals, or went to Church regularly. My mother introduced us to church when we were very young, wanting us to have some exposure so when we became adults, we would have the background and some foundation of God.

When I was 13 my best friend and next- door neighbor asked me to go to her church with her and her family. This was a Baptist church. I went and loved it! I accepted Jesus Christ as my savior, and then later was baptized. I was so happy and passionate about my newfound faith I didn't miss a service. I felt so happy being amongst the many

Christians who belonged to this church, this was like a new family! I continued to go and my love for God grew. I was involved with the youth group, sang in the choir and went to Sunday service every week.

After a couple of years, my parents divorced and my mom, brother and I moved to another city. My church life ceased to exist and I was now faced with a new high school, meeting new friends, and just trying to fit in. Starting over your senior year isn't easy, but I made the best of my situation. My faith seemed to take a "back burner" in my life at that point.

> Isaiah 30:18- "So the Lord must wait for you
> to come to Him so He can show you His love
> and compassion. For the Lord is a faithful God.
> Blessed are those who wait for His help." (NLT)

Graduating from high school was exciting, but going off to college was even more so!! I went away to a small university, joined a sorority and had the best time of my life. Of course I still believed in God, but never went to church. My life was filled with me, me, me partying, studying, more partying, and just hanging out with friends. Focusing on school, work, and my social life, took precedents over anything else, including my faith.

My junior year I met my husband to be. We fell in love and dated exclusively until we got married in March of

1979. Unbeknownst to us, God was putting people in our lives that would affect us and touch us beyond belief!

My husband I were two very strong, intelligent, independent people who didn't really depend on anyone. We were educated, independent and successful in our lives and jobs. Yes, we struggled like most at the beginning of our marriage, but through trial and error, we managed to live a pretty great life. My husband was raised in church his whole life so had a strong belief in God from the beginning. Speaking for myself, I never relied on God for much of anything. I had gotten out of the habit to really include Him and have a relationship with Him. I don't know how and why I did this, for everyone who was important to me I devoted my life to.

The same goes with God in your life. The more time you put in and making God a priority, the better your life will be. But at that time I could handle anything without help, so I thought. I'd pray occasionally for good health and safety for my family and friends, like most standard prayers for a lot of people but never more than that.

Ten years after we married we had our first child, a son! He was the highlight of our lives! We loved and adored him, spending every waking moment we could together. He was such a blessing to us. We knew we needed and wanted to bring Chase up in a "Christian home" so we soon found a "church home" we loved and started going as a family each week. We had Chase involved in Sunday school, summer bible study, mission trips, youth groups, Christian summer camps, you name it, and he did it. We went to church as a family every Sunday, getting Chase involved, but we didn't do anything ourselves outside of Sunday service. We made our presence, tithed and went home. I call it being a "part-time Christian." For me, it was not believing in God, I just didn't make God a priority in my life. I was so busy with my kids and husband and it was hard to squeeze Him into my busy schedule!

Six years later, I gave birth to my daughter, Tayler. I was so happy; I finally had "my little girl!" My own mother and I were so close my whole life; I wanted that with my own daughter! Tayler was one of the happiest little girls I ever knew. She had her moments like everyone, but for the most part she was always smiling. She was very affectionate, loving, and kind and could be mischievous in her own little way. She was my "mini-me!" We were inseparable, doing everything together. I loved shopping for her and with her, lunch together, going to the movies together, doing projects together, fixing her hair for an event, talking about any and all issues that came up in school. Just spending every waking moment with her. She was such a loyal person, loving her family and friends so much. She was the "best friend" and was so devoted to all of her friends, almost to a fault.

She was mine! My son, who I adored, was so busy with my husband and sports. They were always gone to a game or practice of some sort, and so Tayler and I were always together. We never missed any activities with either child their entire lives for they were our lives! We were very loving parents and devoted our lives to our kids 100%.

Our lives went fairly smoothly, a few bumps along the way when my husband changed careers and went into commercial real estate. Because of his integrity, moral background, and drive, my husband was very successful in his business. Eventually I was able to stay home and raise my kids. I knew I was so blessed to have that opportunity, and loved getting involved in all of their school projects, volunteering with parties, P.T.A., doctor appointments, etc. That was my life and I loved it.

Again, to Tayler, I was her "everything" from the moment she was born. She couldn't ever get close enough to me, I mean literally! She had to sit on my lap, hold hands, sleep with me, lay on me; you name it she was on me. (Now I look back and reflect on how lucky I was having her, sharing every second together that we did.) I loved the closeness with her but also at that time was worried her being too dependent on me, which in my eyes was not good for anyone to be, especially a female. I wanted her to grow up to be strong and independent just like me! "I am woman hear me roar" was my motto, I can handle anything and everything. Just bring it on!! Boy was I wrong!

Psalms 91:15- "When they call on me, I will answer; I will be with them in trouble." (NLT)

When Tayler was 10 months old, my husband's sister Peggy passed away at the age of 45. We were shocked and so sad this happened to our family. We had lost elders before this, but this was different. This devastated the family and changed us forever! My father-in-law never seemed to "get over it", which was hard for us to understand. I thought how sad this was, I missed her too, but life goes on doesn't it? We went home, on with our lives, and of course when we would visit my in-laws everything seemed different. A sadness hung in the air. You could see the deep grief in their eyes, never really going away. Not shortly after Peggy's death, my very first "God Kiss" came, me not having any clue if this was even real, so this was confusing to me.

GOD KISS

This was very short and shocking to me, not knowing what to think after it happened. A few weeks after Peggy passed away, she came to me in what's called "a visitation dream" while I was asleep. Now this is not like any other dream I've ever had before. Peggy appeared to me as bright as can be. I only saw her shoulders and up, and she was just as I had seen her last, healthy as can be. The background was black, but she was bright and in color, real and alive! Her message to me was "Ginger, tell my family that I am doing great, and that I love them and miss them." Now this is what a "visitation dream" is. It is very real and vivid and probably something you will never forget. Usually when our loved ones come to communicate a message, they come with a purpose. I believe this is God allowing "the veil" to be lifted between the heavenly realm and the earthly realm, just for a "God Kiss."

I woke up right then, kind of shocked that this happened for Peggy and I weren't real close. I loved her, and we were family, but we basically saw each other usually during holidays. She had her own life in Dallas, and we had ours in Arlington. Why did she come to me? I was always been intrigued by the spirit world, and believed it to be true, but had no idea this would be the beginning to my journey to finding God.

About four years later my father-in-law passed away from lung cancer. "Dado" was a special man whom both my children adored and were extremely close to. Once he went into the hospital, my children never got to see him or say their goodbyes. God blessed us with a "God kiss" regarding Dado and Tayler later on in the book.

Chapter 3

"Death is nothing else but going home to God, the
bond of love will be unbroken for all eternity."
~Mother Teresa~

My daughter Tayler was the epitome of life. She was so
vibrant, happy, and exuded love for just living. She was a
very focused child; seeming to know what direction she
wanted to go in for her life, even at a young age. She was
very committed to her schoolwork, friends, and family and
just about everything she did. She loved to dance and at this
time decided she wanted to try out for the Junior varsity
drill team. She worked so hard every week stretching during
the weeks, practicing at dance class, twirling constantly in
the kitchen or where ever she was. She had her mind made
up, so she was going to prevail for sure.

Once the limping started, we diligently tried to figure
our what the problem was. As we were going from doctor to
doctor, and test after test, I could tell Tayler was feeling very
discouraged. It didn't seem to stop her from going on and

living life, but to be in constant pain eventually takes its toll on you. We still didn't know at this point what was going on, and trying to be positive, I kept encouraging her everything would be fine and not to worry. We had spring break to look forward to and that was always a blast for us.

I was driving Tayler back to school from having blood drawn (another test to see if cancer was involved) and on the radio came this new song by Miley Cyrus called "The Climb". Tayler said, "This is my favorite new song Mom." As I listened to the words, they scared me and made me sad for they sounded like "she knew" and didn't feel she was going to make it. My response was, "Tayler, we all have dreams and we all have mountains to climb, for life is not always easy, but you will make the team and your leg will be fine." I felt she was starting to get down from all she had been going through, and somehow she knew the final outcome.

After I dropped her off back at school, I called my good friend Aleda and was crying. The words to this song haunted me as I replayed them over and over in my head.

"I can almost see it, that dream I'm dreaming, but there's a voice inside my head saying you'll never reach it, every step I'm takin', every move I make, feels lost with no direction, my faith is shakin', but I gotta keep tryin', gotta keep my head held high."
("The Climb" by Jessi Alexander and John Mabe)

I could see in my daughter's eyes, she was scared and worried. I knew I had to be her strength for she trusted me and depended on me to protect her. As frustrating as this was, I had hope all would work out and this would all go away.

Deuteronomy 31:18 - "The Lord himself
goes before you and will be with you; He will
never leave you nor forsake you. Do not be
afraid; do not be discouraged." (NIV)

Putting away this worry, all of the doctor appointments, tests, blood work, x-rays, MRI's, and physical therapy we flew to St. Kitts. We loved the Caribbean so much; we couldn't wait to get away. The first full day we were there, all went well. A little sightseeing, walking on the beach, laying by the pool, and fine dining that night, all was perfect. The second day we did some more touring by convertible and Tayler seemed to be doing okay. On day three, we went into town to do some shopping which was out favorite past time! I could tell on Tayler's face she was struggling a little and really getting tired. That night she didn't want to eat out but order room service and rest. Her leg was beginning to bother her again, and we thought maybe she tired it out from all of the walking we did that day. By morning her knee had swelled up and she was in horrific pain. That's when she and I came back early from our trip to get her in to one of her doctors.

He drained her knee that helped temporarily and then the biopsy was next to come the following week. When we found out she had cancer, we were horrified! Our baby, this was happening to my precious child! The joy of my life, the happy positive little girl, my mini-me! I called my doctor immediately for an anti-depressant for I knew I had to remain positive around Tayler without constant crying. On March 31st, 2009, we get the dreaded call to take her to Children's Medical Center, to the oncology floor. She had leukemia!!!

Well after all of the researching I had done, this was a fantastic prognosis for her! This was the best cancer to have for a child! It was 98% curable!!! Thank you Jesus, we were going to beat this! When I told her we had to go she says, "Mom, do I have cancer?" Both of her grandfathers had passed away from cancer so she knew it lead to death. But with a great attitude I said, "yes you do, but the good kind. It's leukemia and you will be cured!" With trust, she gets in the car and we head to Dallas, she is admitted, they do a bone marrow test and sure enough it is there. But her doctor was shocked! He said, "normally my patients come to me with 100% in their bone marrow, but Tayler is at about 30%!!!" Hallelujah, that was even better than we thought! We caught it early!!

Charlie and I moved into this large family room with her and lived there for the next week. We called all of our family and friends and Tayler's friends to let them know what it was. Everyone is stunned but they are all sending up prayers for her. All across the states we had family and friends, friends of friends, bible study groups, all praying for her. We felt covered and had faith, things will be all right.

James 4:14- "Yet you do not know what tomorrow will bring. What is your life? For you are a mist that appears for a little time and then vanishes. " (ESV)

Within a few days, her friends were coming to the hospital bearing gifts, stuffed animals, banners from school, cards, baskets of magazines, books, c.d.'s, blankets, letters, all for Tayler. She was so happy and felt so much love; she had no idea how much she was loved! Tayler was so sweet and humble, she had no clue that she was beautiful, inside and out and was loved by so many. We decorated her room with all of this stuff, trying to make it a better place to stay.

Tayler had her port put in, and we were taught how to take care of her when we got home. She had exercises to do to keep up her strength, medication to take daily and was to eat as much as she wanted for the treatments would cause her to lose weight. They also told us "if she ever gets a fever bring her in immediately for she has an infection which is very common for leukemia patients." Their white blood levels will get so low their own bacteria will attack their own body. So that was a must to remember.

I took all of my stuff out of my medicine cabinet to put all of her meds in there. It was incredible the amount of prescriptions she had to take. But it became a daily routine and she took them like a champ. I could tell she was losing weight and her disposition was becoming very sad. I felt mental attitude had a lot to do to surviving this, so I tried to uplift her everyday, being very positive and optimistic. I could definitely understand why she was feeling this way. Cancer is scary! For a 13 year old girl to endure this pain and fear of the unknown, was a huge endeavor. It wasn't fair my precious daughter should ever have to deal with something like this! This isn't supposed to be!

For the next couple of weeks, I didn't leave her sight. She slept in my bed where I could be there for her if she ever needed anything. Stephanie, our hairdresser, came over to cut her hair for it was quite long and starting to bother her. I also thought when she did lose it from chemo; it wouldn't seem so drastic if we cut it shorter now. I had already taken her to buy some wigs for when the time came, so we were prepared for that dreaded time. By the end of her third week and fourth treatment they called and told us Tayler was in full remission!!! I came into my bedroom where she was watching television, and I started to dance and sing, "your in full remission" with the biggest smile on my face!"

She started crying, I started crying and we called her dad at work to tell him the great news! We couldn't wait to call everyone and let them know also. Tayler even wrote on her My Space and Facebook saying, "I'm going to live!!"

Now that didn't mean we were finished with treatment. I knew this would last for two years or so, but for this to happen so fast we knew this was a victory!! It never crossed my mind that Tayler wouldn't survive this. She was too young and happy of a person and had so much to live for. We continued to call all of our family with tears of joy! Her friends all wanted to come see her but with her immune system was compromised, so we had to be very careful.

She already had one girlfriend scheduled to come over who went to a different school so we allowed that for Saturday. Taking every precaution with hand sanitizers, she visited for an hour or so. As tired as Tayer was she was really glad Danielle came to see her. Her mom called me after they left and was crying, worried for Tayler for she had lost so much weight. Her little legs were so thin, and Tayler even mentioned to Nyse she was scared about that. Watching your child dwindle down to nothing is a horrible thing to witness. But with cancer, I felt it was part of the whole disease so I tried to put it out of my mind.

By that Sunday, she wasn't feeling up to any visits. I called her doctor who was on call and asked him what to do to ease the pain she was feeling. Her entire body was sore and he said that was normal from treatment. Just give her the pain pills and she would be fine. She got up and out of bed fine, ate her meals fine, but just was sore all over. I massaged her body all day while we laid together watching television. Trying to get her mind off her pain, we watched bridal shows on gowns and I would ask her what kind of gown would she want one day when she got married? We watched movies all day long and if I wasn't massaging her, she was laying on me, snuggling with me and I savored every moment. I called the doctor's office throughout the day and the same answer to help her was to continue giving her pain pills. She didn't have fever, so pain pills was all I could do to keep her comfortable.

By 11:00 pm that night, she couldn't sleep. She sat up and said, "mom I can't sleep I still hurt!" Out of frustration, I got out of bed and said, "I don't know what else to do Tayler, I'm calling the hospital and we are going. They can figure this out!" She was so weak at that point she couldn't walk to the car. Her dad lifted her up and put her in my car. I drove her to the hospital and we checked in that night. They hooked her up to all of the monitors, gave her pain meds, and watched her all night long. Her blood pressure was dropping, her heart rate was dropping, still no fever but they couldn't figure out what was wrong.

Finally at 2:00 pm that next afternoon, the doctor came in and said they were moving her to ICU so they could figure this out. They had an entire staff that would monitor her and find out what was going on. Before we left our room Tayler had to use the bathroom. She had zero strength to even get out of bed, so I had to lift her and get her over to the portable besides her bed. She couldn't go and I thought maybe she was nervous, so I told her to wait until we got her upstairs. If I had known what was really going on with her I would have realized her kidneys were shutting down!

They did blood work and sent it off to pathology and the doctor said "we are going to treat this like an infection. We don't know what this is, but the antibiotic will kill whatever it is." Before they put her to sleep, we said our goodbyes, kissed her and said "we'll see you in the morning." Her eyes were scared but she knew we loved her and trusted us in everything we decided to do. About five minutes into the surgery the surgeon came out very quickly and said, "the blood sample test came back and it's septic shock! We will treat her but will have to see how this affects her organs!" What?!? What does that mean?? Of course she will be fine! This is normal for leukemia patients to get infections; she will be fine, right? The surgery went well, and the doctor told us "we won't know for a couple days or so to see if her organs are affected by this so for us to go home and get some sleep. I wasn't going to leave so I told Charlie to meet me here back in the morning.

By 2:30 am that next morning I woke up thinking it was time to get up and meet Charlie at Tayler's room. I realized it's still too early and so tried to go back to sleep. Around 3:00 am a nurse calls me and says "how fast can you get here, your daughter has gone into cardiac arrest!!!" I throw on a robe, call my husband and frantically tell him to get here as quick as possible. They tell me if I want to I can go in her room where they are doing CPR and have been for about 30 minutes. I decided to wait until Charlie gets there. I give the nurse my sister Kathy's number to call and let her know.

Charlie runs into where I was and we hugged and I'm telling him "she's in cardiac arrest and they are doing CPR!!" They take us in her room and I will never forget her face. Her eyes were opened and I knew she was gone. They continued to work on her for another 45 minutes and Charlie and I continue to plead with Tayler to please come back to us! "We love you Tayler, fight honey, you can do this! Tayler please, mommy and daddy love you, please Tayler?" We finally told them to stop, and with pure exhaustion left the room with our heads down. We walked into the waiting room and there were my sister, my son and his girlfriend, and our closest friends. The first thing I said was "she's gone! My baby is gone!!!" I couldn't believe this really happened, I was numb and walking around shocked. We all cried together for they all loved Tayler too and were stunned this even happened.

We talked to the Chaplin before we left and then went into where Tayler was to say our goodbyes. She was so beautiful and at peace I didn't want to let her go. I cried and hugged her, then Charlie and Chase. We walked out after everything was complete and we drove home. Numb, exhausted, tearful, and in shock, we left our baby girl at this strange place alone.

> Job: 14:5- "Since his days are determined, the number of his month is with you; and his limits you have set so that he cannot pass." (NASB)

"A Butterfly"

A Butterfly
lights beside us like a sunbeam
and for a brief moment its glory and
beauty belong to the world but then it flies
again and though we wish it could
have stayed… we feel lucky to
have seen it.

~Unknown Author

Chapter 4

"There is sacredness in tears. They are not the mark of weakness but of power. They speak more eloquently that ten thousand tongues. They are messengers of overwhelming grief… and unspeakable love."
~Washington Irving~

Going home and stumbling into bed is all I could do. I took something to help me sleep, crawled into bed with Tayler's stuffed rabbit she had at the hospital and passed out. I have no idea how much later I woke up, I just did. It all is such a blur to me right now, trying to remember the events that took place. I do remember people started to come to our house that afternoon.

Friends, family, strangers, old and new poured into our house. Bringing water, food, and supplies to sustain us for no telling how long. I had no idea who some of these people were, they were just there, helping out, pitching in where needed.

When one of my girlfriends came in, Cynthia, I remember going to the door as she entered and saying "Yeah, God really listened to all of the prayers from people who prayed for Tayler! It didn't matter she died anyway! He didn't save her! If God is real, why didn't He save her?" I was furious, crying and blaming God for not saving my baby girl! She never hurt anyone she didn't deserve to die! She was all about life and love! She was too young to die! What kind of God let's precious souls die young?

Hour after hour more came to hug us, cry with us and see if there was anything they could do for us. Condolences, flowers and cards came constantly for weeks. We were astonished with all of the love that came through our door.

That week our pastors John and Betsy came to visit and we discussed and planned the funeral. What in the world are we doing? This isn't happening, burying my child? Picking out a casket, a burial plot, which is now for the entire family, a time and date, arrangements for music, where family is to sit!!! This is such a nightmare, when am I going to wake up? She's only 13 years old finishing up 8th grade! She was going to be at the high school this next fall, taking driver's education to learn how to drive! Summer is about to start and vacations, sleepovers, water parks and just having fun!!!

Leading up to the service, people came in and out of our house non-stop. It was a very good distraction from reality, almost like this was people just visiting us. A lot of tears, but comfort also. We were so busy with the arrangements, people visiting, phone calls, family coming in from out of town, the reality of this whole thing was not thought of. When the day came for the service, it was a somber morning, family all in, getting ready for this horrible day.

First came the day of "viewing", and a lot of Tayler's friends came for that. They would approach her casket with tears and sadness, hard to understand why would a young girl like this die? The reality of death hit them square on. Tayler, was always so pretty and vibrant, and always with a smile on her face. Always the one to brighten one's day or help someone out at school. Tayler loved color so she dressed beautifully and girls copied her style! She was a role model for so many and now she was gone! They never got to see her again and say their "good-byes". This was a very devastating moment in their lives.

The next day was Tayler's service. We all arrived early, greeting family and friends who were in a special area together. When we entered the sanctuary, the place was packed. We sat in the front with family and close friends near, and the service began. It was all pretty much a blur to me, but one thing I clearly remembered was Tayler's best friends at one point stood on stage and all read a letter to Tayler. They were all so stoic and brave, reading their personal, and beautiful letter aloud. Not a dry eye in the house, and they all got through it with so much strength. They wore bright colored dresses and converse tennis shoes for that was Tayler's trademark, in a way. She owned many colors and wore them every day.

After the service we went to the cemetery for the ceremony there. Hugs and tears, so many kids from Tayler's school, family and friends were all there to support us. It was a beautiful, sunny day and I know my baby girl was with us, smiling down at the turnout for her. She was so humble and precious, she had no clue how many people truly loved her.

Psalms 116:15- "Precious in the sight of the Lord
is the death of His Godly ones. " (NASB)

We are going through the motions, just surviving each day. Without thinking about reality, the food and people kept coming for weeks. I can say I felt that was such great help for me for I could talk and talk, reminisce, laugh and cry and never really have time for reality to sink in. It was all so surreal to me and I didn't really believe this just happened to us. Even with all that we had done to prepare, surely Tayler was here, around with her friends and this was someone else's nightmare!

About a month after everything started to die down, the distractions stopped, the visiting ceased to that extent, and reality hit us. When everyone left and our house was quiet, the "knife" turned in my heart and I felt such intense physical pain. I couldn't stop crying and feeling such despair. Walking around like a zombie, barely sleeping, barely eating, just basically getting dressed and wandering around. I went through such intense anger towards God for all I was told most of my life was "God can heal, and cause miracles!" I was a good person and mother, things like this just didn't happen to people like me. We loved each other, were a happy family, we we're Christians! So where was He when hundreds of people were praying and Tayler still died? What kind of God allows this to happen? Or, is there a God anyway? Or was Tayler in the doctor's hands and at their mercy? I went back and forth with these two scenarios, struggling with the fact "what if there really wasn't a God after all?" I felt like a small child having a temper tantrum, stomping my feet, falling on the floor, crying uncontrollably. I was begging and pleading with God to please bring her back. I would live homeless, naked, if He would give her back to me. (If you knew me, naked in front of the world to see is a huge sacrifice for I'm extremely modest!) But that's how desperate I was. I would trade my life for hers. I was 52 years old, I lived life long enough, give her a chance to at least live as long as I have.

We would see life still going on around us. How could that be? Our daughter just died!! How can everyone still go on with laughter and happy lives when we are suffering and in pain!!! We didn't even want to leave the house and didn't for about six weeks. We couldn't stand the thought of running into someone who did or didn't know and having to rehash what we had been through.

After weeks and months of begging, pleading and bargaining with God, I remember being on my knees, face to the floor, praying to God and begging to please take this physical pain inside of me away. I couldn't bear the knots in the pit of my stomach anymore, living with the sick feeling inside of me, day in and day out. The next morning when I woke up, miraculously it was gone!!! I was totally astonished and amazed and thanked God for helping me. That small blessing helped my faith grow from that day forward.

> Matthew 17:20 - "You don't have enough faith", Jesus told them. I tell you the truth, if you have faith even as small as a mustard seed, you could say to this mountain "move from here to there", and it would move. " (NLT)

GOD KISS

This visitation dream came to my husband Charlie a week after Tayler's service. Charlie's dream was identical to Tayler's service. After it was over, we walked up the aisle holding hands and our heads were down. About half way through the sanctuary Charlie looked up and his father stood up from a pew and their eyes locked. He looked to be about 35 years old!!! The sight of him made Charlie wake up immediately. He felt this dream was for him to remember! (Remember Charlie's father passed away 7 years before this occurred at the age of 70 years old.) I believe this was Charlie's dad telling him that he knows and is now with Tayler. My daughter loved and adored Dado so much, I know she was so excited to see him when she passed. That was a huge comfort for me knowing they are together.

Chapter 5

"The pain is nothing to the joy of meeting again."
~Charles Dickens, Nicholas Nickleby~

Through this journey you go through so many stages and they seem to go around and around, repeating themselves. First for me were shock, then denial, next bargaining , anger and depression, and finally acceptance. This road is so long and intense, you can't rush it, speed it along, or forget it away. By this time now, I'm so angry at the doctors I write them a letter stating they ruined my life, neglecting my daughter, and therefore she died. (I now switched my vengeance towards her doctors instead of God.) I knew it was someone's fault, and I had to figure this out, get some answers, if I was ever going to get some relief from all of this pain. Surprisingly enough, her main doctor called and for some closure, we went into talk to him. I did leave feeling better and was told it was basic protocol for how she was treated. Without fever they were confused with her situation so they did what they felt was right at the time. You can make yourself go crazy asking "what ifs" all day long. A different doctor, a different hospital, should we have put her in an environment at the hospital to escape all of the germs? Now this was reality, our baby girl was gone and we now have to figure out how to live without her.

The best way to describe this for me is to have a limb amputated. It is part of your flesh and blood, you had it from birth, and it was part if you. Now that part of me is gone, I have to learn how to function without it. Tayler was my life. My existence came from getting up and getting her up for school, helping with homework, school projects, dentist appointments, being with her on and off all day long. It continued after school until bedtime. We had such a deep love for each other; she was part of who I was. She was my mini-me, and pride and joy. We loved shopping having lunch out, dressing up for any occasion getting manicures and pedicures, going to the movies, talking about everything, just spending time together. To lose that was and is like losing myself. Who am I now? I lost my identity, my reason to live, the point of my existence. She needed me, my older son really didn't anymore, nor my husband really, for they were both independent and self-sufficient. I floundered for many months, not knowing what to do, how to live again?

The world lost its color when Tayler died. I felt so lonely and empty, what's the point of going on? I never was one to ever think of "killing" myself. I never felt anything in this life was worth ever doing that. But now I feel different. She was my life, and now she's gone. How will I ever fill this hole in my heart again? How will I continue to go on living life without her? How will I ever be truly happy ever again?

Psalms 6:8 – "And I believed the Lord…
Heard the voice of my weeping." (NASB)

GOD KISS

Nyse was Tayler's best friend and Tayler came to her first. The same week Tayler died, the visitation dream took place in the Bahamas where we all went together the summer before Tayler passed away. Tayler was sitting by the beach crying. Nyse went up to her and just cried with her. There were no words spoken but when she hugged Tayler, she said, "She felt so real!" Tayler had stopped crying, but of course Nyse still continued. Tayler continued to hug her, laying her head down on her chest while Nyse cried. The next thing Nyse remembered her father waking her up for school and the way Nyse was laying on her bed, she noticed a "tear" on the pillow next to her where Tayler would normally sleep. I've read there is not crying or sadness in heaven, but I believe even though Tayler is with God and family, her life here was precious to her, and I have to believe she misses us here too!

Part of my therapy, dealing with this every day was journaling my feelings. Betsy, our grief counselor, pastor and our angel from heaven, said, "Every time you feel sad, write it down." Well that was pretty much everyday for a very long time. I couldn't seem to function very well at all, so this helped. I tried to jump back into life, staying busy, hanging out with friends, going to the movies, trying to resume my old life so I didn't feel the pain. That did not work. I realized you couldn't go through something this painful and meaningful and "move on." Facing reality is the only way to survive this horrific event in my life, not running from it. Taking one day at a time.

Charlie and I were like "ships passing in the night", both just stumbling around the house, both numb. We were there for each other, but yet in our own world of grief. Everyone grieves differently, but at this point we were at the same level, just shocked and confused. It's so surreal to think this had actually happened to us. We couldn't grasp the reality of our situation. I felt like this was a bad dream.

In the meantime, I read nonstop, books on life after death, anything about heaven, parents who'd lost a child, Christian books, just trying to find some answers. This helped to keep my mind focused on something positive and something to look forward to that reality. The thought of seeing my daughter again was my only hope in survival at that time. I wasn't ready to read the bible, or even go to bible studies. I wasn't ready to be in a group where it was too close and personal. I still couldn't go a day without crying, and that was way too early to be involved in the "God stuff." I still was on the fence about the reality of God at that point anyway. But I loved His promises and believing in eternal life. It started to come around, slowly but surely.

We went to church every Sunday, but that was extremely hard for that was where Tayler's service was held. I would look down at the front of the church and see where the casket was. But going gave me strength, hope, peace and knowledge, listening to our Pastor John talk about God and having faith.

Before this I was always a person who loved life. Had an incredible family, was so blessed with amazing friends, retired from work at age 35 so I could stay home to raise my kids, and was a very positive and happy person. I had somewhat of a foundation of faith from when I was very young, but as I aged I became preoccupied with life and busyness, therefore, my faith was put on the "back burner". I always believed "things happened for a reason" and in fate. But after this death, I struggled with the "whys" in our situation and trusting God. It just didn't make sense to me why someone so precious and young would die? I know this happens everyday, probably every second of the day, but that's other people. Not us, the happy family who wanted their children, the ones who had great lives!

But going through this tragedy, we found people coming into our lives to help us through these things. My girlfriends were there for me in a heartbeat. They would just drop over, call me daily, include me in stuff they were doing, bring some food and wine and they would just let me talk away. My college sorority sisters would come and spend the night with me. Sleepovers even at 52 years old were fun. They listened to me while I laughed, cried and shared my stories with them.

My daughter's best friend Nyse and her family became our family now too. We were inseparable. We try to see them weekly for dinner, and they are part of anything and everything we do now. And what's strange, a lot of these women who I am great friends with now didn't happen until after Tayler passed away. I knew them all, for my daughter was a friend with their daughters. So we basically would drop our girls off at each other's houses and wave goodbye. My daughter had a great sense of good and bad, right and wrong, I trusted her to discern if they were good people or not. But that's how God works, sending people to you in need. They now have blessed me beyond measure and I love them all dearly.

Another amazing thing that has happened are Tayler's girlfriends, still to this day come and hang out with us. From the very beginning, these girls have been by our side this entire time. Every birthday party, just call to come over, stop by on a weekend, texting me a sweet message, or celebration we have concerning Tayler, they are there. There are usually 10 or more who always come to share in the memory of my daughter. They still want to come over and have sleepovers here at our house and these girls are graduating seniors of 2013! That is a true blessing and a reflection on how blessed we are with such amazing friends and with Tayler's friends, who are also now like daughters to us.

You will see throughout this book, the God Kisses are from my adult friends, my husband and many from Tayler's friends. God is giving me these gifts to strengthen my faith in Him. And boy is it working! Thank you God and glory be to God!

GOD KISS

Lauren E., (Tayler's friend) had her first visitation dream with Tayler. She said that the six girls that spoke at Tayler's funeral were in class crying. For some reason I came to each class and took them to the gym. (The gym was where they all met before the bell rang in the morning.) They sat in a circle and were talking and crying when in came Tayler! She sat down in between Lauren and Nyse and she said to everyone, "love all of your family and friends, and enjoy the fun times, because that's what I remember when I think about you!" Nyse replied, "I'm scared and I miss you so much!" Tayler said, "I miss you too, but be happy and enjoy life!" The last thing Tayler said in this dream was "please help look after my family!"

This dream made me extremely happy to know my daughter is still around us. It sounded just like her to say, "Help take care of my family." She was a very nurturing little girl, always taking care of others if they weren't well. Each time she had a cold or something to keep her home from school, she was so appreciative I took care of her. She would say, "mom, thank you for taking care of me" and she would hug me so hard. What a precious spirit she had!

These dreams and signs helped me so much trudge through another day. People would see me and say, "Gosh you are doing so well, you seem so strong!" But yet inside I was dying. On the outside I looked strong and holding up, but on inside I was a shell of who I once was. This continued through the first year of this journey.

One thing I couldn't do was go to the cemetery where Tayler is buried. I wanted her close to our home, but it kills me to go there. My husband finds peace and comfort there. He goes every week to put fresh flowers on her grave and cleans up our family plot. I just cry, for I know her little body is beneath us, and I want to dig her up and take her home with me!! It kills me!!! I know her spirit is not there, but her physical body is, and I can't stand to think that.

For some reason, I felt once we got through the first year, it should be smooth sailing. Time heals? Right? Wrong!!!! The reality of our situation came slamming into us like a Mack truck!! She's not coming back! She's not at summer camp, or sleeping over at Nyse's house!! She didn't go over seas to study abroad, or busy with drill team and school! The reality of it is she's really gone from our lives forever. Never to see her again here on earth!!!! Oh my God, where are you? I can't do this alone, and I need you in my life!!

Even though along the way I saw God do some amazing things during this time, noticing so much more than I ever have before, my faith was and is a "work in progress." You have to remember, this is a journey I was called to go on. It's my own, none like no one else's. I have to walk with God everyday to see who He is and what's my purpose. There has to be something more to life than, we were born and then we die. We are buried, turning to dust, and then the cycle starts over. We all have different journey's to travel, and different purposes in life. We will all go through some sort of struggle and suffering. It's not because God is a cruel and mean God, it's so we will all depend on God throughout our lives. This is what I am learning as I travel this long road of pain and suffering.

> Philippians 3:12-14- "I am not saying that I have this all together, that I have it made. But I am well on my way, reaching out for Christ, who has so wondrously reached out for me. Friends, don't get me wrong: by no means do I count myself an expert in all of this, but I have got my eye on the goal, where God is beckoning us onward to Jesus. I'm off and running, and I'm not turning back! (MSG)

Amazing Grace

"Amazing grace, how sweet the sound,
that saved a wretch like me...
I once was lost but now am found,
was <u>blind</u>, but now I <u>see</u>."

Chapter 6

"I suddenly saw that all the time it was not I who
had been seeking God, but God who had been
seeking me. I had made myself the center of my own
existence and had my back turned from God."
~Bede Griffiths
Clergyman quotes~

Going through life now is a struggle. Even with so many around us who love us, they still leave and we are left with the pain we carry with us every day. The memories come flooding back, that horrible night that will be ingrained into my brain forever. I want to live a happy life again, but is it possible? How can I ever be happy again without my daughter? She was my life, like I said before, my identity. Now all I have are pictures, her things like her clothes, cell phone, I-pod, stuffed animals, her make-up and perfume. All left as it was before this happened. I go up to her room and the pain returns; I catch my breath as I wander around looking at everything. Her clothes all color coordinated in her closet, her Uggs on the floor by her many colored converse tennis shoes. Her athletic shoes with her socks still stuffed inside them from cross country running, and her make-up bag on her sink with her photo I.D. for school.

I can't believe this is real. Her bed's made and her room is neat, so she's probably at a friends hanging out, maybe doing a school project with a classmate. Your mind plays tricks on you and you go into denial. I tried to function every day, living like nothing had changed, and I guess that was survival mode. But the dark and deep sadness would creep up on me at some point in the day and knock me down once again.

> Daniel 6:10 – "We stand tallest and
> strongest on our knees." (NASB)

What do I do now? I need help, and hope, I need peace in my life to withstand the rest of my life. I had never been one before to depend on anyone, so this was new for me. Our church provided grief counseling which we went to every week for the first year. Having someone who was "religious" and helping us from a spiritual standpoint would be great! She can tell us facts and answer questions!! I know there will be an answer to our daughter's death? It should explain somewhere in the bible!

Having someone to talk to, rant, rage, and cry our eyes out to, was so helpful and healing. The comfort Betsy brought to us, the hope we felt each week, helped us until the next time we saw her. Her wisdom and spiritual understanding gave us so much peace and kept us taking "one more step", one more day forward. We also found talking to others who had lost a child was very helpful to us.

Betsy told us about Compassionate Friends which is a national organization for people who have lost children. I would highly recommend you try this grief group. We were desperate trying to find some solace, week to week, trying different groups and this one truly understood our pain. Between seeing Betsy and going to this once a month, we had somewhat of a routine to take on each day with some hope. It wasn't of course going to change our circumstances but help us heal with connections of understanding. No one truly knows what to say to you, even if they are your family or your best friend, no one knows what we are feeling. So then you hear comments such as, "God needed another angel", "she's in a better place", "time heals all wounds", "she's no longer suffering, and you wouldn't want that." Noooooooooo, please don't tell me these things!! I want my daughter back!! I don't care if God needed another angel!!! She was a gift to me! I gave birth to her and she was mine! I would lay down my life for my child, trade places with her, go through whatever necessary it takes to get past this hurdle, but please don't take her from me!!

GOD KISS

Mother's Day weekend in May 2009, about five moms, and about six of Tayler's friends stopped by bringing cards and flowers for me. I was touched for this was the very first holiday without Tayler, and it was mother's day on top of that! They all stayed all afternoon visiting, eating, the girls were in and outside having a ball. About 9:00 pm that evening, some of the mom's started to clean up the trash. Rhonda got a large trash bag and gathered it all up and went out to the garage to dump it. Now she's in real estate and has been in all types of houses, so when the garage door light went on, she thought it was on a timer, so proceeded to walk to the far corner of our garage. We had three vehicles inside and mine was in the middle. It's a small two-seater, convertible, and then next to mine was my husband's large SUV. As she walked back towards the door to the house, she passed my car and from her peripheral vision she saw movement inside my car. A very fair skinned arm was resting on the console. Around the wrist was a very plain and thin black band and the clothing was very neutral in color. Rhonda said her heart was racing at this point, and soon thought about the light going out anytime if it's on a timer. So she walked around the front of my husband's truck and glanced back to my car to look through the front window to see further who that could be. She said the reflection from the light over my car caused a glare; therefore she couldn't see anyone clearly. She rushed inside and kept this information to herself. We said our goodbyes, and Rhonda went home and discussed this with her husband. About a week or so later, Rhonda came back and she said, "I have something to tell you and Charlie about." She proceeded to walk us through the garage, remembering and retelling every detail about what she saw. The amazing thing about this story is our garage lights are not on any timer. You have to push buttons to turn the light on and know which one is just for my car, for there are six buttons on a panel. The light came on over my car only! Tayler also always wore a ponytail holder around her wrist at all times. I believe this was Tayler telling her to tell me; she was here on Mother's day, celebrating with us!!

> Jeremiah 29:11- "For I know the plans I have for you "declares the Lord"; plans to prosper you and not to harm you, plans to give you hope and a future." (NIV)

How does this not harm me Lord? This just killed my soul, killed my life as I know it! Why would a loving God who has great hopes and plans for my life do this? I struggled with this daily, still trying to find God, feel God and trust God. I really didn't know Him before, but do I really want to now? How can I trust Him when this happened? I had two choices as my pastor John said,

"You can be bitter or get better." My whole life before was always better, happy, bright and positive. Now, bitter seemed the easy way to go. I experienced something no parent would ever wish on his or her worst enemy, and I had to figure out how to deal with it. Do I want to live in misery until my last breath or do I want to be happy, and live through my daughter's eyes, which was all about life and happiness?

Because of my personality, I chose happiness, but how would I do that? Just trying to "act happy" was difficult. Entering back into life was a struggle, pretending I was coping and doing okay was so difficult most days. Betsy would say, "take one day at a time", and in reality, that's easier said than done. My mind was consumed with missing Tayler. I want all of her stuff around me but yet it is a constant reminder she's gone. Never to be seen again here on earth. Never to wrap my arms around her and tell her "I love you", never to share problems with again, help her with her homework, take her places with friends, have sleepovers, graduate from school, get married and have children!! Oh my God, why her? Why my family? She was so precious and had so much life left to live!!

That's where my desperation to have God in my life took place. I knew I could not continue living like this forever. I wanted to feel peace and have hope to even live each day from now on. I know quite a few people who have gone

47

through this before I have and they are surviving, happy, living to their fullest, surely I can too?

Each week during our counseling Betsy would ask, "Where have you seen God this week?" As I would reflect back on the days, I would always see people who were there for me for whatever reason, or see something beautiful that was done for me. A person would call me for help, or a song would come on that was Tayler's favorite. I remember feeling so depressed and upset while driving my car one day, "I Can Only Imagine" came on the radio the minute I turned on my car. (That song was played at Tayler's service). When you truly have your spiritual eyes and ears" open, you start to see and hear things you never would have noticed before. That's how God works, by sending people to help you, signs and dreams, and by giving you these moments of His love and kindness, letting you know He's with you always, as well as your loved ones who are in heaven.

GOD KISS

One hot summer day in June 2009, my son Chase was driving to the Winstar casino in Oklahoma, which is about 45 minutes away from us. As he was driving, he noticed his thermostat was on "hot?" He didn't think much about it, so he turned it back to "cool" and continued on.

About 15 minutes later it was back on "hot" again. Okay, now he's thinking about some of these signs and God kisses we'd been getting and remembered when Tayler would ride with him in his car, she would slyly, when he wasn't looking, turn the thermostat to "hot" when it was summer outside! So now this thought was on his mind, but he turned it back to "cold" and made a mental note that he did. He stopped at the gas station right before he reached the casino to make a pit stop, and before he got out of his car he purposely looked to make sure it was still on "cold" before he got out. When he returned to his car and started his car up, it was again on "hot"! "Ha-Ha Tayler," he said for now felt this was her doing this to him! She learned from the "master" (her brother) how to be mischievous!

These "God Kisses" that continued coming, helped me so much during this journey and God knew my faith and that I needed these to grow in Him. He also knew I needed people to help me along, so He was putting people in my path. One of my neighbors, who I didn't know before brought flowers to our doorstep after Tayler's service. A year or so later I was invited to come to a bible study class in my neighborhood, and this was at the house from the woman who gave me these flowers. At that point I felt ready to be amongst these women and start to study about God. They have touched me and helped me beyond measure, and are huge in my healing and journey to getting closer to God.

Tayler's friends continue to bless us. Some people find it amazing we even want them around us. Doesn't having them around sadden you? Doesn't that make you see what you're missing? Yes and no. Yes, because we are watching them grow up. But the love we have for them, only brings Tayler's memories to their fullest. We had a blast with Tayler's friends; loving every time they came over to have a sleepover, just hang out for the day. These girls still come, just to be with us. They love being in her bedroom, running up and down the stairs, jumping on her trampoline, spending the night here and watching scary movies. All the things we did when Tayler was still here. That alone is a God blessing in itself. These girls could easily have other plans, have boyfriends, jobs, or just not interested anymore, but they don't when it comes to being with us. They could want to move on, not remembering the sadness that goes along with this, not wanting to talk about her anymore. But they don't. They come with open arms, eager to be with us for one more celebration or just being together.

Some of these girls have come to me for advice. Someone other than a peer, to talk in confidence, and just the need for someone to listen. I loved that for I felt like I was talking to my own daughter. I miss that with Tayler, so that helped me a lot. Again, God put these girls in our lives many years ago when we first moved here, knowing Tayler's destiny and how much she would affect our lives and the entire community.

Going to church every Sunday, bible studies, volunteering, doing anything and everything with our Church, gave me such peace and help to heal and learn about God. I began to see Him everywhere, through people, through the beautiful nature all around, through now little things I used to overlook. I am like a child with my eyes and heart opened, seeing the world for the first time with such love and gratitude. I appreciate life and what's all around me so much more.

GOD KISS

I was driving home from Nyse's house and she called me and told me that she saw Tayler's silhouette next to me in the passenger seat of my car! I loved that knowing Tayler is with me as much as she can be! That night Tayler came to Nyse in a dream. She said her words to Tayler were "I miss you and wish you were here with me." Tayler said to her "I miss you too, but I am here with you all of the time!" As you will notice as you read these God kisses, that they are not memories, or normal dreams. These are conversations and interactions with Tayler, just like she was still here on earth.

I'm not going to lie and say this is "a piece of cake", and just having faith will make it go away. This is the worst and hardest thing I've ever experienced and wouldn't wish it on anyone. I used to hear "God only gives you what you can handle!" Really? God, I was kidding when I said "I am woman hear me roar!" I wasn't really that proud and strong!!! Can't you think of any other way to bring me closer to you?" I always felt after my kids were married and on their own, I would then get involved with church, volunteering, bible classes, etc. That's what "older" people did once their kids were raised!!

Evidently that wasn't God's plan for me. He knew the impact Tayler had on hundreds of people, and he knew my heart. He knew what needed to be done to bring people to Him, including myself.

Am I saying God did this to my daughter? God is a loving God and I believe He knows the full story behind this loss for us. He will only bring glory out of these ashes. The more time I spent studying "His Word", the more I learned about who God is. He started to come off the pages and reality sink in. God is real, living thousands of years ago, and still today. The incredible miracles that happened in His name, the people He helped and cared for. Spreading the gospel to others with such love and compassion. Giving his life up for us even though we are all sinners and don't deserve it. The prophecies that came true, 500-700 years before Christ was even born. The bible consists of 66 books, written by 40 different authors, over 1500 years ago, in 3 different languages and on 3 different continents. Yet many of these authors never knew or collaborated with one another in writing these books. Also, these books share a common story line of God's universal love for all of humanity, and for all who repent of their sins and follow God with all of their heart will have eternal life. How does that work if God is not real? There weren't libraries back in the day to do research, to copy someone else's story to make it sound good! These were written by men from all walks of life, at different times and different places and compiled together at different times.

> Isaiah 42:10 – "Fear not, for I am with you;
> be not dismayed, for I am your God; I will
> strengthen you, I will help you, I will uphold
> you with my righteous right hand."

Losing Tayler affected so many people around her. She changed hundreds of kids in her schools, both who knew her and many who didn't. She changed the lives of our friends and their families. She changed our community. That's when I can look at this and see this is not all about me, my loss. She changed so many people for the good, and that alone makes me so proud of who she was. So I have to thank God daily for her life. Even though it was for a short 13 years, it was one of incredible happiness, and fulfillment that I would never change one minute of.

Knowing how much I loved Tayler and for this to happen, I truly believe "God does have plans for me, to prosper me, not to harm me, plans to give me hope and a future. "Jeremiah 29:11. He knows the "big picture" and I have to trust Him in what that is. Once you start to learn about God yourself, you will see that "death is our final gift to God." It is not something horrible to Him, but a celebration that we finally made it! We are complete and finally with God, having eternal life with Him! Have you ever heard the phrase "the good die young?" That is so true. My daughter had completed her journey, had fulfilled her purpose, and now is in heaven living the life we all strive for. I found God, and I do trust Him with all of my heart and soul. He is my God.

This has been a long journey so far, trying to go through life differently. Not dwelling on "what was", but living for "what is." That doesn't mean I will ever forget my precious daughter Tayler, it just means to keep my focus on God and His promises. I find myself still reading daily, praying daily, trying to go on with life, for I have no clue what His plan is for me? I have found comfort in helping others, especially parents who have lost a child, for going through this I know exactly how they feel. Maybe this is my mission now? My strengths are talking to others, listening with compassion, having empathy and sympathy to help someone. Well here you go! I have found myself talking now to others in my situation, and consoling them, listening to them, and crying with them. God does bless us with gifts so that we might bless others.

GOD KISS

Summer of 2009, Charlie, Chase and I were watching home videos. We love to do this occasionally, for there are so many great memories on them. This particular one was at Christmas time. Tayler was opening one of her Santa gifts and was showing me when the door chime went off. That will happen when someone opens one of our doors in the house. Chase had just been outside so Charlie said, "Chase did you not close the door good enough? Possibly the wind blew it open?" Chase said, "yes I closed it when I came in." Charlie got up to check the doors and they were all closed tight?! He went to check the alarm system pad to see if a light was blinking to show us which door was ajar and that's when he noticed "the chime" was turned off!! Charlie had turned it off when he went out that morning to get the newspaper. The chime went off when Tayler was talking to me and showing me her Christmas present when it went off! Tayler was letting us know she was with us at that time. The door chime has never done that again since.

Another God Kiss came from a 4 year old boy, and his innocence and trust is just precious. Nyse has twin cousins and she and Tayler would babysit them on occasion. Caleb loved Tayler and was very protective of her, never wanting to leave her side if Tayler was over. Caleb came to my house with Nyse after Tayler had passed away. It was a couple of months after her death when Caleb brought up Tayler. Out of the blue he said, "Tayler comes to see me all of the time." Nyse said, "Really, what does she have on?" Caleb said, "duh, Tayler clothes!" Nyse said, what does she say?" Caleb replies, "She tells me she misses me and loves me!" Incredible! I love that!

The next visitation with Caleb came a couple months later and Caleb asked Nyse "why did you change your bedroom to the one across the hall?" Nyse said, "Because I wanted to have a bigger bedroom." Caleb said, "no it's not the reason, Tayler said you changed because you were tired of sharing the bathroom with Alex and he clogged up the toilet all of the time!" Hilarious!!! Besides being shocked of this visitation, Nyse and Alec laughed hysterically for exposing the truth!

The belief and trust of a child, how precious! This is just the beginning and God has shown me so many of his amazing mercies, so I would see Him and grow in my faith. Each and every one of these have helped me so much, taking one more step closer to healing and to loving and depending on Him. I know that now I am seeing Him so clearly, and appreciate daily my life, and my family and friends. I am so blessed!

"My Life In You"

I can never give thanks enough for all
you've done for me,

my life has changed for the "good",
and now my eyes can "see",

you're in my heart, throughout my soul,
my old life died away,

because of you I'm free at last,
to live joy throughout my days.

~Ginger Reynolds~

This was written to God along my
journey.

Chapter 7

"People see God everyday,
they just don't recognize Him."
~Pearl Bailey~

My foundation of faith was on sand before. I had a great and fairly easy life, and always in control of all of the outcomes, never truly, in my heart depended on God for much of anything. I had strong faith in my husband and myself, but not so much in God. So when this major storm hit me, my life fell apart. I felt so hopeless and desperate for the first time in my life, homeless. Finding God in the midst of all of this rubble helped me rebuild my life from the ground up. I now have faith built on a rock, which is God! It doesn't mean I won't experience any "storms" in my life again, it just means with God in my life, I can withstand all things that come my way. He weathers the storm with me and gives me hope, peace and strength knowing I will survive.

I am still having a difficult time dealing with Tayler's death. The days are becoming a little easier, and the pain is subsiding. As time goes on I seem to handle the days better. I try to keep my mind positive and focus on what is good in my life instead of dwelling on "what was". I try to focus on God and heaven, and seeing Tayler again for I can't change reality, so I have to look forward, taking one day at a time. "Doing" positive things really helps with healing.

When you study the word of God, you see how the disciples all suffered throughout their lives by following Jesus. Why am I any different? Boy was I naïve to believe just because I was a good person, loved my family, and was baptized; I would be safe from real tragedy. This happens daily and I always believed it would be some other family this would happen to, not me? I read about it in the obituaries, but that was again someone else. God would protect me because I accepted Him as Lord years ago, surely I'm safe, but that is not God's promise to us. What he wants is a personal relationship with Him and for us to "need" Him. If everything were perfect, why would any of us need God?

At this stage of my journey, I am managing better, having somewhat of a schedule, but still not really pushing myself out of my comfort zone. I want to stay safe in my home, not going out too much and for too long. I haven't really committed myself too much, just trying to stay above total depression. Starting a bible study class at our church really has helped me learn about God. Slowly, I opened up to His teaching and wanted to soak up everything I was reading. This takes time for there are so many meanings in scripture, and you can't take everything literally. But the more I dug in, the more I got out of it and understood. I truly fell in love with God. It's very simple like I said, love God and help others.

> Galatians 2:20 - "I have been crucified with
> Christ. It is no longer I who live, but Christ who
> lives in me. And the life I now live in the flesh
> I live by faith in the Son of God, who loved
> me and gave me himself for me." (ESV)

Having God in my life has changed me, literally from the inside out. Your old self dies and you are resurrected into the "new you". You "see" things so differently and notice everything. What once made you happy is now shallow. What once made you laugh is now at a higher standard. You don't "sweat the small stuff." Yes, I am more sensitive and compassionate like never before, but then I also see people for who they are.

When you lose a child, life is magnified. Sadness, love, happiness, anger, impatience, betrayal, selfishness, friendships, all is exaggerated. It puts life in perspective, showing what is important in life. You see for the first time the true character of people you once tolerated. Not because I think I'm better that anyone else, but when you are in such intense pain you can't handle any other stress in your life. Plus, when you depend on other "people" for your happiness, you will always find disappointment. Only God can fill you up completely with complete happiness and trust. People come into your life for a reason at that time. But now I know there are "seasons" for people to come in and out of our lives. God has a plan for all who crosses your path, when and why, so trust in Him and things will always turn out for the best.

GOD KISS

Summer of 2009, Christine N. had a visitation from Tayler while she was outside one day and had fainted. She said while she was unconscious, she saw Tayler standing over her, holding out her hand and was calling her name! Christine came to shortly after that!

God has brought me so much peace and joy. I never understood how this could change my life and really affect me, and all around me. Being "religious" seemed so boring to me before, stuffy, and too traditional, way too many rules to abide by. Who can live by all of these rules, laws and commandments? Years ago it was way too restrictive, closed minded, judgmental and condemning to me. I'm going to hell anyway if this is how we must live and be!

I had way too much fun and enjoyed my life to follow all of these rules. But that's not what accepting Jesus is all about.

Faith" is about following Jesus. You have to have an open mind and heart for growth. It's about loving God with all of your heart and soul, helping others, and being the "light" to bring people to Christ. I have two very good friends who I've known from college. Gail and Mitzi, even at 18 years old, were followers of Christ back then! They radiated with love and joy and I would look at them and think, "Really? Are they for real? They just seemed too sweet and happy!" But they were and still are today the same incredible Christian women.

You know that movie "When Harry Meets Sally" and a woman says, "I want what she has?" Well, that's me today. I want to be that beacon of light for others to come to me for help, comfort, or friendship. The pain is so intense losing a child, helping others helps take that pain away, a distraction from your own problems, to helping others. That is pure joy to me and knowing that I can bring peace, hope and the offering of love through Jesus Christ to others.

GOD KISS

My daughter adored Susan Simmons. It didn't surprise me that she came to her one night in her dreams. This is Susan's recollection. "About three months after Tayler passed away, she came to me in a dream. In it, I was standing at one end of a basketball court that I recognized as the middle school that she attended. It seemed to me that it was early morning, before school usually starts and there were kids hanging around talking. In front of me I saw two girls talking. The girl facing away from me had long blond hair but it wasn't until she turned around that I recognized her as being Tayler! She didn't say a word but just smiled. In an instant I was struck by how wonderful she looked. My only words to her were "Tayler! You look so good! You look like you did before you were ever sick." She smiled even bigger and the dream was over. The next morning I woke up thinking, "you dream about Tayler and that's all you could come up with to say to her"? But the fact was that she did look good, like she had a quality to her beyond health, beyond beauty. She had an ethereal quality to her that is hard to describe. And the happiness on her face made me feel ecstatic! It took me a few days to tell Ginger about the dream because I didn't want to remind her of Tayler's illness but ultimately I knew that she'd love to know her precious little girl was absolutely perfect now!"

Once I realized God had been in my life the entire time the more I could see that more clearly. God does give us "free will" to make choices, and now I can definitely see those choices I made without any regard for Him. We were all created for a purpose, leading us to glorify God. God gave us all gifts, and once we recognize them, we are to use them to grow His Kingdom.

A very dear friend of mine, Marsha, who I met at one of our "Compassionate Friends" meetings (she lost her son before I had lost Tayler), said to me one day, "I feel so blessed God chose me to glorify His name!" In other words, she looks at the death of her son as a privilege to her, for God is using her for His glory. At this point in my journey, I'm not there yet. I wish God would have chosen another way to use me to glorify Him, but that wasn't my choice. I do know I've always had the gift to gab, and when I'm passionate about something, I can talk about it forever. God is my passion, and will be until I take my last breath, for now I know He is real, heaven is for real, and His promise for eternal life is real. I have to share that with all I know! I want everyone to see God and know He is alive and waiting for us to "open our heart" to Him. With God in our lives and the promise of eternal life, how much better can it be to see our loved ones and be together for eternity!

1 Corinthians 2: 9-10 "However, how it is
written: "No eye has seen, no ear has heard,
no mind has conceived, what God has
prepared for those who love Him." (NIV)

Knowing God's promise for eternal life, and all of the God kisses I've experienced at this point has helped me immensely. We are all suppose to believe with our heart, even though no one can comprehend the magnitude of God and heaven. That is what is called "Faith". You believe in what is unseen. It's not logical or black and white. It's God. Our brains can't even begin to understand how this all works. The one thing I do know, God has changed my life, and I want to get to know Christ, as I grow stronger in my faith.

I look back now as a mother and wish I had been a better role model for my children. Yes, I loved and adored my kids, but being the person I am now is what I should have been during their young and developmental years. "Walking the walk" instead of "do as I say, not as I do", would have been a much better way, so they could've seen Christ through me. Yes, I always was involved in their school, volunteering, room mom, PTA, and just helping out where and when I could, but having a loving "Christian" heart would have made a bigger impact on them. I pray now my son will see who I've become and hope it's not too late to be a great influence on him. I know my daughter is smiling down from heaven proud of me, saying, "Mom, you go girl!"

GOD KISS

We went to or first JV football game. Tayler was to try out for the drillteam, and so in her honor they dedicated a dance to her. They presented me with flowers and a card that night. It had been storming so the game was delayed. The game was starting at about 9:00 pm, so was very dark outside. Right before the game was to start, the drill team girls were yelling and laughing for me to come see the double rainbow!! I walked around the side of the stadium and there right in front of us was the most beautiful double rainbow!! It seemed to be within 100 feet from us. All of the girls were hugging, crying and laughing and saying, "It's Tayler, and she's here with us!! " Now remember, it's pitch dark outside and there it was in all of it's glory! I was blown away, but not surprised Tayler was with us!! As we walked around the corner to sit down for the game, the most beautiful sight came into view. On the other end of the stadium was a large hole in the clouds. The clouds were bright from the light shining through the hole. Inside this hole were colors of pastel blues and pinks. I felt I was looking into heaven!! It was gorgeous and very spiritual to witness. Again, it was nighttime and to see something like this was only a gift from God!

Chapter 8

"Example is not the main thing in influencing others.
It is the only thing".
~Albert Schweitzer~

Getting more involved now, I see helping others is so vital along a Christian journey. With who I've helped so far regarding others who've lost a child, the gratitude I feel not only from those I talked to, but also the feeling it gives me, one of peace and healing from God. It has helped me heal so much just being there for another person who is struggling as I am, and to share our journey together. This is a "fraternity" I would have never chosen to be in, but it is a group of people that all have a common bond.

I always loved to listen to others, trying to help if all is possible, but this is different. This has a much more deeper meaning than anything else I've experienced. Like I said before, the other things I used to fret over and worry about are now so trivial. But God knows if your heart is into what you are doing. Just showing up, putting on that smile, and going through the motions, is so empty and pointless. You might be fooling those around you for the time being, but not God. We could call ourselves Christians, but without truly loving God and helping others, we are just fooling ourselves.

GOD KISS

Kelsey W., (Tayler's friend) sent me an email to tell me Tayler and her visitation dream! She said she was at our house in the basement (we don't have a basement), and down the stairs came Tayler! She said she ran to her and hugged her, seeming like 5 minutes and the hug was so real! She told Tayler, "I miss you so much and wish you were still here!" Tayler said, "I'm here all the time with you and I will definitely be here for Halloween!" She then told Kelsey to help keep all of the girls together as friends. Halloween was a huge holiday for us, for we would have the most amazing Halloween parties for all of Tayler's friends and a sleepover. I believe Tayler also could see the girls separating somewhat because of school, and wanted Kelsey to help keep their friendships going.

Finding God is one thing, but maintaining a relationship with Him is another. So many people say they are Christians but never "open their heart" for Christ. Once you set your priorities to have God <u>first</u> in your life, the need and want of having Him close to you is so strong. You will want to learn all you can and study "The Word." You will have the desire to get involved with helping others, join a church, go to bible study, being part of the Christian life, being the hands and feet of Christ. The time you put into this relationship, the more you get out of it. This has been so important in my healing and going forward with living.

Dealing with the second year without Tayler has been challenging. I can't pretend anymore, and I can't change anything but myself. I have to take my life and make it the best possible. I thank God everyday for my daughter's life, remembering not to fall back on the pain. I want to live my life through Tayler's eyes, for she was all about happiness, love and life. I know she wouldn't want me to live being sad, but to go forward and being grateful for my life. That's why I have to stay close to God, for He is the only way to achieve this kind of goal with this kind of tragedy.

Sometimes I feel guilty for wanting to see and be with Tayler more than Jesus. But now I know God gives us those yearnings to awaken us to Himself. When someone we love is in heaven that becomes more real and vivid. God created me to love to this depth, and it's normal to have these desires and longings for those we love.

The joy I feel today, versus how I felt before knowing God is totally different. Happiness is the emotion that is temporary and expressed on the outside. Joy is the emotion you feel from the heart, which is from God! Trust me, losing my daughter is the worst and hardest thing I've ever had to live with, and to find joy again is only from God. I never ever thought I would even want to live, but to feel this joy and contentment can only come from God. He alone can do this for anyone who lets Him dwell in his or her heart and soul. A living, breathing journey is what faith is all about. We are all saved by the Grace of God!

> Philippians 3:8 -"What is more I consider everything a loss compared to the surpassing greatness of knowing Christ Jesus my Lord, for whose sake I have lost all things. I consider them rubbish, that I may gain Christ." (NIV)

You know one thing I find astonishing is that Jesus died for us all even though we are all sinners. He died a criminal's death because He loved us so much, taking every sin upon himself so we could have eternal life. To receive this amazing gift of salvation and forgiveness of our sins is to trust in Jesus Christ as our Lord and Savior. To think I could have a new beginning, regardless of my past, and He does forgive me, just proves the love God has for all of us.

Some of you may already have the Lord in your lives and I am so thankful for that. Those of you who don't and are still struggling and angry, what are you waiting for? It's a shame I had to lose my daughter to really have a relationship with God.

If you want Jesus Christ in your life and to take the step toward true joy and happiness, you just pray this prayer:

> Heavenly Father, I repent of my sins so please
> forgive me. I believe Jesus Christ died on the
> cross to save me from my sins and give me
> eternal life. I ask you Lord Jesus, to come into
> my heart and be my Lord and Savior. Amen

Now is the true test. Do you want to be a Christian and have pure joy in your heart and life? Or do you want to call yourself a Christian, show up for Sunday service, go home and live your life independent from God like I used to? You can't go back to your "old life" and expect anything to be different in your life. Christ lives within, so unless you make changes to yourself and make this a priority, it will all be in vain. It takes work like in anything that is worth fighting for. Your marriage, job, and your friendships all take work, loyalty, and commitment to keep them strong and good.

Yes, I am a "new Christian", and very passionate about Him and my new life, but I made a promise to myself and to God to NEVER live without Him again. I've been on that side and I know that life. I know that feeling of emptiness; even with all of the wonderful "things" and people I have had in my life. Just a constant chasing of filling that void that seems to haunt us all if God is not in our lives. I have an amazing husband and son and still am so blessed with an abundant amount of friends and family who love me and care for me very much. But to have God as number one in my life, to have the Holy Spirit alive inside me, guiding me, everyday, giving me that inner strength and joy, I will never live without that presence in me ever again.

GOD KISS

September 13, 2009 Maddie E., (Tayler's friend) moved to California, and like a lot of new students trying to fit in, was having a tough time fitting in her new environment. Going into 9th grade, she said she had been crying a lot and felt unwelcomed for a while. One night, her visitation dream was with a group of girls, and no one could hear her. (That was symbolic for feeling left out.) She looked over to the side and saw Tayler smiling at her! She all of sudden felt Tayler's presence and the girls' acceptance of her. She whispered to Tayler "thank you" and then Tayler was gone. That was just like Tayler to help one of her friends out!

Tayler was so compassionate and sweet, I can see her doing this without hesitation!

Now that I have a better understanding about faith, and having God in my life, I am excited to see what He has planned for me! I have to trust in the Lord, and know he loves me and has great plans for my life. I do know helping other parents who've lost children is one of my missions, but what else? I will wait patiently and see what God brings to me through my journey. I can't wait!

> Romans 8:28 - "And we know that God causes
> all things to work together for the good for
> those who love God, to those who are called
> according to his purpose." (NASB)

Chapter 9

"Healing does not mean going back to the
way things were before, but rather allowing
what is now to move us closer to God."
~Ram Dass~

When you go through something this difficult, the loss of
your child, it's so hard to even want to go on living, let allow
being happy and positive. Just know this "healing journey"
will be one that will take the rest of your life. There is no
"quick fix" for this; just taking one day at a time is really
all one can do. If you dwell on the past, you will only live
in depression. If you look too far into the future, you will
feel anxiety for what "should have been." Until you focus
on today, will you eventually feel joy again.

What I am going to share with you in this chapter is
not only my God kisses, but also the steps I took towards
healing, and trying to live my life through my daughter's
eyes. Remember, she was all about life and living, therefore
my choice is to live the best possible way I can, for the rest

of my life. You have to face reality, deal with this death, and the only way to do that is head on, to move forward, one step at a time, and one day at a time with that in mind. This will never go away, and "stuffing" your feelings and your pain will only postpone it for later. It will come out eventually, or eat you alive. I chose dealing with it, living with it, and surviving through it.

One if the major things we did to help us on our healing journey is counseling. We went to our church and got grief counseling through one of our pastors. My husband, son and I did this together for over a year. Sharing this session helped us all with the cold hard facts of this reality, but also being together as a family, helped us immensely. That helped us through week after week, seeing with spiritual eyes, the love and Grace God has for all of us. You will never get the answers you want, but you will get the peace that you need to survive. We still continue to this day, going every other week and it's been over 3 years now. How long is long enough? Until you feel it's been long enough, until you can live life again with a peaceful mind and heart.

Another thing I did which was very therapeutic for me was creating photo albums of my daughter's life. I bought an accordion file and went through all of our family albums of pictures we had taken throughout her life. We also had bought Tayler a camera for her last Christmas, and fortunately for us, she had taken over 300 pictures of her and her friends! A lot of them were of her, by herself, taking funny pictures in her bedroom. So precious and I'm so happy she had that camera! I then organized them by category: birthday, school, parties, holidays, artwork, family, etc. From there, I bought scrapbooks, all kind of stuff to decorate each page with, stickers, letters, etc. I ended up making three books from her birth to her final pictures at age 13.

More people, including her friends, love to look through these books and reminisce. Even though I cried along the way, I also smiled, laughed and enjoyed the journey it took me to complete them. I started them 2 months after her passing and worked non-stop to finish them. This was a very happy project for me, reliving so many memories that I had with my daughter.

I now feel the need to help other parents in this same situation. This is something I need to do. Since I have this experience now, I've had numerous calls about other people who need help because of their loss of their child. No one can soothe you like someone who's walked in your shoes. A very dear college friend of mine wrote me on Facebook telling me about one of her friends whose son died 4 months after my daughter and asked if I minded contacting her to talk to her. I did immediately and we bonded instantly. We were each other's sounding board, to cry to, rant, yell, talk about happy memories, just sharing our children with each other. Without knowing her before, I flew out to Arizona where Lynda lives and stayed with her 3 nights. We had a great time, feeling like we'd known each other forever! It was wonderful to be with her and we continue to share our sadness and happiness together.

Again, another way to heal is to help others in the same situation. We are the only ones who truly understand the pain we suffer. Friends and family of course are great, but it's still not the same.

The first year after Tayler's death, I slowly started to go to a bible study at my church. The group was large enough where I wouldn't have to really talk to anyone. I just wanted to study and absorb as much as I could, learning about God. There are so many parables, passages that are symbolic, signs, and hidden meanings, that reading it alone was a real challenge to me. Being in a group, discussing each verse, dissecting each passage really helps understand. Of course, this will help you understand and learn about God, but to have God in your heart, means you have to open up your heart and mind, accepting Him as your savior. Just studying is not enough. Living by God's word, becoming Christ-like is what it will take to have a complete life in Christ. This bible study has been a huge step toward my love and life for Christ. Getting to know Him personally is the only way to thoroughly love life again, living again, and finding your purpose in life.

Isaiah 40:31 - "But those who hope in the Lord
will renew their strength. They will soar on
wings like eagles; they will run and not grow
weary, they will walk and not be faint." (NIV)

As time passed and I felt the nerve to be around more and more people, I felt called to sing in the Praise Choir at our church. I've always loved to sing since I was a little girl. From choir in school, to college sorority contests, I loved it and was always involved. I felt God's hand leading me in that direction, therefore, I got my courage up and now sing every week. This is a smaller group but the bonding and love for Christ, just radiates off the stage with these people. The love they have for the Lord is so present; you can't help but feel such joy being amongst them. How much more can one glorify God by worshipping Him in choir on Sunday? I can feel the Holy Spirit move in me and that makes me so happy, bringing tears to my eyes.

Going through life now is different doing positive things like I've mentioned so far, is how I chose to go forward with my life. I can't seem to get enough of our Church. The people are incredible, loving and so supportive to us, it's unbelievable. We have been so blessed to be a part of this magnificent church. I volunteer as much as they need me, wanting to be the servant to Christ now. He has done so much for me my whole life, now it is my turn. I can never repay Him for all He's done so far. I am now on the "Mission Committee" so am involved with the missions our church is involved with. It's so rewarding to see all what is going on behind the scenes. To be with such a large church, I am proud to say it is one of love, kindness, integrity, true caring of others, and an incredible church staff. I am honored to be part of it, helping others, which is part of loving Christ. That's what life's all about!

GOD KISS

You will see I have dedicated a chapter to "spiritual orbs." I truly believe they are our loved ones in heaven. They have shown up in many pictures not only that we have taken, but from various cameras and friends along the way. They are not in every picture we take, but seem to be in every picture pertaining to Tayler, be it her birthday celebration, sleepovers, Christmas celebrations, or just hanging out with Tayler's friends. She is with us! In late fall of 2009, this particular dream was my very first one I knew was from Tayler to me. That evening, my son Chase and I were watching the news and there were two young guys shooting hoops in their backyard. The amazing thing about them, they took shots standing up on their fence. From every angle in their yard they made these amazing shots. Well, my visitation dream was I was watching these two young guys shooting hoops when all of a sudden an "orb" floated in my vision catching my attention! I watched it float by until it stuck on the backboard of the basketball goal. Out of that orb floating towards me were very large initials, T M R!!!! These are my daughter's initials to her full name!! I believe that was her way to say "mom those orbs you keep seeing in your pictures are me!!! I am always with you!!! I woke up immediately with a smile on my face and said "thank you Tayler!"

One of the hardest things I think we do is to celebrate Tayler's birthdays and all holidays without her. For the first birthday after Tayler's passing, we had all of Tayler's friends over for a sleep-over, dinner, movies, took them to the water park, everything we did with my daughter, we did that day. The very first birthday was so sad and hard, but with all of the girls with us, we had a "bittersweet" celebration. It was so strange to go through the motions, have everyone there, doing the same things as usual, and my daughter not there. But that made it tolerable. After dinner we went out to the cemetery to release balloons. Tayler loved color so we had rainbow color balloons. It was very emotional but I'm glad we were all together during this time.

The next big party we had with all of the girls, was our yearly Halloween party. This was one of Tayler's favorite holidays and had a blast planning and preparing for this day. We didn't have "cute" stuff, but scary décor. My husband was amazing at decorating our house from top to bottom. From music, to old black and white scary movies playing, to spider webs, clowns with horrifying masks, anything ghoulish, you name it we had it! We really struggled on doing anything that first Halloween, for everything was still so fresh. To have as much fun as we did in the past, we knew it would be difficult to put on that face and make it fun for them. So we decided to do a smaller version of our normal Halloween parties.

We only decorated the upstairs game room (you will see a picture in the "spiritual orb" chapter), and I had creepy food and snacks. We took the girls to a place that has 5 haunted houses and made the evening there. The pictures we took, there were orbs everywhere!! Being Halloween eve I don't know why I was surprised. A lot of spirits were there at this park! One of the workers who led us through the beginning of this one haunted house said to us "okay Tater-Tots" follow me this way." What? Who says that at a Halloween Park? Tater tot was my daughter's nickname by many of her friends. That was strange!! They stayed the night and we watched scary movies together. These girls are amazing and made this celebration happy considering the reality of the whole situation.

"Trials and tribulations build character.
Character is what we all need to support
the destiny God has planned for us."
~Unknown~

Now Christmas time is something I wasn't looking forward to. To my family, this is a huge celebration for us. We went way over board on gifts, too much food, a lot of family, but we loved it all. I would start to shop for my daughter early, really out there all the time, buying something for her whether she needed it or not. My mom and I shopped a lot, and I carried on that fun tradition. Now, that hole was huge in my heart and to have to deal with this holiday without her was going to be a big challenge. This is such a depressing time for us; we really just wanted the month to go away. We cancelled our family dinner at our house, not wanting to even celebrate anything. How will we be able to smile and enjoy anyone when our family is incomplete? Everyone else gets to move on, get together with his or her loved ones and enjoy the holiday!

One of the things we did, and continue to do is light a candle every day, the entire month of December and put it by her picture. That way she is "with us" during this holiday and part of our celebration. We had to do things differently too. The old family traditions didn't work anymore, for they brought about too many memories. So we had to create a "new normal." We now go to a Church service on Christmas Eve morning, focusing on the real purpose of Christmas and then come back to open presents with my son. Just doing that made it feel different, therefore, we handled it okay. From there we went to my mother in laws to visit family. We enjoyed the family away from our home, but didn't want to be in our home, where too many reminders were. Out of sight, out of mind really helped for the moment.

Another thing I did during the first Christmas holiday was make a "Grave Blanket." I learned about it at another "Compassionate Friends" meeting. This is greenery you can make or buy to lie on the burial place of your loved one. Because my daughter loved Christmas and had her own tree, I decorated this greenery with whimsical, bright, colorful ornaments that she would have loved herself! With a big bright red bow on top, it turned out great. I'll never forget when I was first making it, my friend Laraine called me and said, "What are you doing?" My response through tears was "making a grave blanket for my daughter!!!" I was still mad about my situation and couldn't believe this is what I was doing. Everyone else was having fun with their families; doing the normal stuff you do for Christmas! I was mad, sad distraught, and depressed. My emotions were so fragile and raw; I very easily would go through these huge mood swings. I just couldn't wait for this month to be over with. Then my life would start over with a new year and surely be better?

GOD KISS

December 2009, my husband, son and I were at the nursery to pick out our flocked Christmas tree that year. This was a family tradition we all did together, but this year was of course sad we went through their inventory quickly, picked out the one we wanted and went to pay at the check out center. I realized I forgot white lights so we all went down the aisle where they were sold. As we were looking the song "The Climb" came on!!! Okay this is Christmas time, with Christmas music, in a nursery, and this song came on? This was played at Tayler's viewing service and was one of her favorite songs!! We all looked at each other with huge eyes and couldn't believe that happened! That made me smile for sure! It just shows our loved ones are with us all the time!

Another God connection that happened to us during this time was a family consisting of a single dad and his 13 year old daughter, brand new at our church, needing help with everything, car, job, home and with Christmas. Yes, I know there are many who are in this same situation, but when Betsy, our grief counselor told us about them and wanted to know if we wanted to help with their Christmas, we were honored. What are the odds of a 13-year old girl, without her mom, needing help at this time of year, at our church? We jumped in with both feet, providing them everything they would need to have a great holiday! What a blessing that was for us, to focus on them, helping them instead of dwelling on our own situation. Again, very bitter sweet for me, for I got to shop for this teenage girl, buying her things I would Tayler. This helped me with my pain and sadness, thinking of them, sharing with them that first Christmas holiday.

To this day we still have not gone through my daughter's clothes or changed anything in her room. Everything is the same, and I still struggle with doing that right now. I have already gone through her jewelry and bagged up individual bags for all of her closest friends. I know Tayler would've wanted them to have her stuff, and I knew they would cherish it too. One idea I was given about her clothes was to make them into a quilt! I loved that idea because I knew I would not be boxing up 150 pieces of clothing and moving them around with us. I couldn't just give them away to anybody who would eventually just throw them away. We will eventually be settling into a smaller house, and then will be forced to face her room and making those changes.

I believe by that time, we will be able to do that without too much anxiety and sadness, handling it better. I know its just "things", but a big part of her was the way she dressed. She had such a great eye for fashion, dressed adorable, and always was very creative with her style. She wanted to be a fashion designer, therefore, took great care on her appearance. Of course, I created that little monster, for having a Fashion Merchandise major for a mom! That was our "thing" and she reflected it completely! So it's a little more than just stuff to me and this last step will be completely surrendering her to God. I know Tayler is in heaven, so much better off then even myself, but she was my baby and this challenge will take me a little longer to complete.

GOD KISS

On January 22, 2010 my friend Rhonda and her daughter Lauren had the same visitation dream the same night! Rhonda called me and asked if we could meet for lunch one afternoon, so we did and that's when she told me. She said she walked into a restaurant and saw a very long table with a white tablecloth on it. She walked over to it and started to look around and from a distance she saw a girl sitting at another table with an older man. Her hair was back in a ponytail, and Rhonda thought, "That sure looks like Tayler from behind." All of a sudden, the girl turned around and it was Tayler!! She stood up with the biggest smile on her face, waving to Rhonda, and that's when Rhonda woke up!! She said she was shocked to see Tayler alive and looking just like she did before. Next, Rhonda's daughter Lauren comes downstairs for breakfast before school and proceeds to tell her mom that Tayler came to her in a dream last night! Rhonda is in the pantry now getting lunches together, and she said her heart was racing, listening to Lauren describe her dream. Lauren said "I walked into a restaurant and saw this long table with a white table cloth on it. All of the other girls came in behind Lauren, (we always traveled with 8-10 of Tayler's friends for any get together), and they all came up to this long table. Lauren said she looked around and noticed this young girl sitting with an older man, and she said she looked like Tayler with her ponytail. The girl turned around and stood up waving and jumping up and down, so excited to see everyone there!!! All of the girls ran over to Tayler and started to hug her. She described Tayler wearing a hot pink scarf and a purple top and Tayler said she had just gone shopping and bought her entire outfit!! She said she was very happy and loved heaven!!!

Okay, explain this. Mother and daughter having the same dream, the same night!?! That is not your brain just working and doing incredible things to help you. Believe now there is a heaven and there is a God who orchestrates all of these things in our life!!! God gave this gift indirectly to me, through my friends and Tayler's friends. That's how amazingly God works! Thank you God for all you've done for me. You know what and when for things to happen in my life, and I trust things will all work out for the good!

One thing everyone has to face is the anniversary of their child's death. The first anniversary was so hard and depressing, and very emotional. My saving grace for that day was Tayler's friends' skipped school that day to spend it with me. My husband wanted to spend that day at the cemetery and our church alone, so I stayed home all day, safe in my house. When everyone came over, I put on home movies of Tayler when she was a baby. They made everyone smile and laugh, seeing how cute she was with her older brother. My niece came by, bringing me a basket and a gift, flowers were delivered to us, and my friends stopped by throughout the day. Having them with me helped me so much deal with this horrible day. This was a day I wanted to go away quickly.

Along the way, Charlie and I decided to donate a fountain to our church in my daughter's memory. Now this is not a small garden fountain, you might think it to be, but one of great majesty. We had no idea what we wanted, so my husband began to do research and he found a picture of the most beautiful Jesus statue you have ever laid your eyes on. We made the decision we wanted to make an exact replica of this statue and put it in the center of the fountain. We had to scale the fountain according to his size. The statue is 8 1/2 feet tall and is the center of the fountain. The total height is 18 feet high and it's 30 feet across. From there, God began to work through all of the plans, putting people in the right places, connections with different companies, you name it, the pieces started to fall into place beautifully.

My husband went to China three times while the marble was being carved, coordinating all of the work and people that took place to build it. This was a major project that took 1 ½ years to complete. Watching the process was like a tapestry being created by the hands of God. To reflect on this now, I can see how all of the pieces came together so beautifully and perfectly.

We had the dedication in June of 2011, revealing the beauty of it to the church and all who wanted to attend. It's not only our church's fountain, but the community's. We want this to be a sanctuary for people to come for peace, reflection, solitude, or help for any problems they may be experiencing. There is something so peaceful about the sound of water, "living water", and when you look up in the eyes of Jesus, you feel the over whelming sense of peace. We now hear people coming up to us telling us how much they love the fountain and how it's helped them so much. It's healing others and that alone is a great feeling to have, knowing that Tayler's life was not in vein, but one of purpose.

Something we never considered when building this fountain was "what to do with the money thrown in? Betsy and Dara approached us and asked us what we wanted to do? After some discussion, we came up with "Tayler's Water Wells For Africa." How perfect is that, monies from our fountain to drilling fresh water in Africa. Who would have thought we would ever be involved in anything like this!!

Now, this is our new mission and we plan to go to Africa to start this process. Besides drilling a well, our Pastor John also wants to build pavilions to serve as a school, church or clinic nearby for these people. This will be another huge project for us, but again we are excited to go and get this started. Putting our sadness into something this beautiful and positive can only bring a smile to our faces! We can't wait to travel this journey now, open to any and all possibilities this will lead us to!

GOD KISS

On January 27, 2010 I had turned off the light and TV to go to sleep. Charlie turned over and said "what light is still on?" I looked up to see if I had turned the TV off completely, and it was off. So I rolled over and Charlie said "there is a light still on in our room?" I sat up and looked around and then noticed the stationary bike was on. It's computerized and so a light comes on when turned on. Charlie is the only one who uses that and he hadn't been on it for 3 days!! The button on the bottom is very hard to push, and our cat didn't turn it on! My mind went to Tayler giving us a sign that way. I smiled and turned it off then went to sleep. About 2:00 am, my husband woke up, wondering if my son had gotten home. He walked past the alarm pad and noticed the alarm was still set. Charlie went to check and see if Chase had come in when the alarm went off!! It was so loud, I sat up in bed wondering how long it would take for him to turn off. When it finally went off he came back to tell me Chase still was not home, and the alarm went off by itself!!! We don't have any motion detectors, so that was not the cause!! Tayler is in motion again! Little stinker!

As you can tell I don't believe in coincidences. Believing in God makes me realize things happen for a reason. He has a plan, a master plan for us all, and when we focus on Him you will see as things unfold, that are meant to be. I read in this book a wonderful quote about coincidences. The book is called "I Saw Heaven" by Patti Miller Dunham and the quote was "There are no coincidences in life. They are actually small miracles where God chooses to remain anonymous." I love that! Even though I would have never chosen anything like this to ever happen, like I said before,

God knows the end of my story. There is a great plan and reason for all of this pain and suffering, and I believe with all of my heart, the end product will be a beautiful tapestry of my life to withhold. I am serving the Lord, studying His word, and trying to live my life through my daughter's eyes. Surely I can do this for God, myself and for her. I know Tayler is smiling down on me, so happy and proud of my journey so far!

"The Serenity Prayer"

God grant me the serenity
to accept the things I cannot change;
courage to change the things I can;
and wisdom to know the difference.

~Reinhold Niebuhr~

Chapter 10

"When we embrace the many parts of our
experience we discover a magnificent creation.
Every moment is but a thread, a thread of
consciousness embracing the very essence of life.
Some threads are brilliant and dazzling while
others are tattered and torn. When looked upon
in isolation, the tattered threads look inferior.
Yet when woven together by the wondrous
hands of the Creator, the light magically blends
with the dark. As joy coalesces with pain, God
creates the magnificent tapestry, that is life."
~Debbie Milam~

I find it amazing, now with my spiritual eyes and ears, how I can see how my life fell into place. It never, ever crossed my mind that I would marry my college sweetheart, have two beautiful children, and then one would die. Even when Tayler was in the hospital, did I ever believe we would lose her. But through all of that, I can now look back and see when people were put into my life and how their impact on me was part of my journey.

One of the first incidents that happened over 30 years ago, was about a sorority sister of mine who's brother David, was killed in a car accident. Months before this accident, I had asked him to dance with me in a dance marathon for our sorority fundraiser that year. He was a good friend of mine, so he happily danced with me that night. David was a in the Sigma Chi Fraternity, as well as my <u>future</u> husband Charlie. (Charlie and I didn't really know of each other at that point.) The night David was killed, Charlie was the first one to be on site when it happened!! First "child" I knew to die, my friend, my husband's fraternity brother, and Charlie being the first to see the accident, and my husband to be! Barbara, David's sister has been so supportive and comforting to me through my journey. That connection was only a "God thing."

Along my life, I have had four friends who have lost a child, two friends who had lost their brothers, one friend who lost her sister, my sister-in-law died at the age of 45, and even my step-sister lost her infant son. I never really put these together for any reason other than "how sad for them", and then went back to my life. I never saw God in much of anything, for my faith for most of my life was inadequate. Again, "I am woman hear me roar" mentality is what I went with my entire life.

You can say life happens, people die everyday, everyone knows someone who dies? But this is out of sequence, out of the norm for a child to die before the parent. This is what makes this so hard to deal with. I've been to many funerals so far, and losing an elderly person of course is sad, but living a long life is the natural state for most. But to lose a child, is beyond what a parent can deal with alone.

> John 3:16 - "For God so loved the world, that He gave His only Son, that whoever believes in Him should not perish but have eternal life." (ESV)

As I had stated earlier, people come and go in your lives. During this time in my life, I saw all of the people I had known through the years, come forward, loving me, supporting me, and carrying me through this pain and suffering. The people in my life know us now as survivors and are people who appreciate the tough times, as well as the happy times. I can share with them, laugh with them, and cry with them. They don't avoid me when I call, but seem to cherish our friendship that much more. This has also changed them, having a much stronger and meaningful faith, so they see life through tears, but also hold onto the beautiful and happy times they now experience. These friends seem to know when to listen, and when to give me space. Thoughtful cards, an invitation out to lunch, dropping by on a whim are all thoughtful things true friends do.

I have learned now to be there for others through horrific situations like this. Not just "go on with life", but be supportive and compassionate so they have someone to fall back on. Before, I took life for granted. Life was rosy for us, so I didn't worry about much, always knowing "we could fix it" if ever needed. My family was healthy and in a safe environment, no problems, no worries. Boy has life changed for me!! Life means so much more to me. I laugh harder, I cry harder, I appreciate my family and friends so much more.

For 25 years we lived in one city, where both our children were born. Uprooting them because of safety reasons, we moved to a beautiful and much safer place. We loved this community and felt this was the best place for our children to grow up in. I became particularly close to two women, Susan and Aleda, but also had many "angels" who were there for me throughout this journey. Some I never knew, and some became friends long after the fact. From old friendships, to new ones, to college sorority sisters, to my fantastic family, from our church, bible studies, to organizations I belonged to, I was surrounded by people who truly loved me. I believe this was God putting His arms around me, steadying me before this "blow".

GOD KISS

May 30, 2010 my husband Charlie goes to the cemetery every Sunday to put fresh flowers on Tayler's grave and clean up around it. This particular Sunday it was very cloudy and dark with clouds covering the entire sky. It was approximately 4:00 pm in the afternoon when had finished replacing the flowers and cleaning up. He then went to sit down behind this small building a few feet away. He looked up into the sky and noticed a bright opening in the sky that reminded him of what we saw one night at the first J.V. football game we had gone to a year ago. As he was thinking about that night while he was looking down in the grass, he clearly heard Tayler's voice say, "Dad, look up!" Charlie looked up in the sky, and there was another opening in the clouds that formed a perfect large circle. Within that circle was Jesus Christ sitting on a throne looking down at my daughter. Tayler who was on her knees was looking up at Him!!! Charlie said he could see her features perfectly, and also of Jesus Christ's. The details were like a picture ,His long hair, beard and robe and Tayler's facial features and her hair were all so clear. Charlie was not having a dream! Remember, this was at 4:00 pm in the afternoon and he was wide-awake and coherent! The image lasted for approximately 20 to 30 seconds before disappearing. This was an incredible gift to my husband, and for all of us to hear! God wants us to know Tayler is perfect and well with Him!!!

Now, just to clarify, my husband has always been a good Christian, very smart, a realist, and always had common sense. To witness something like this is amazing. If someone else had told him this story before losing Tayler, he would have had strong doubts and thought they had a screw loose in their head. This gift was given to him to also give him peace in knowing our baby girl is well and with our Heavenly Father.

When I think about the struggles up to this point, I realize how much I am loved. I had always heard "if you can count your friends on one hand, you are lucky." Meaning, if you have at least 5 friends, you are blessed. I am abundantly blessed! God has given me so much love through other people. I count myself very fortunate.

> Philippians 4:8 - "Think about things that
> are pure and lovely, and dwell on the fine,
> good things… Think about all you can praise
> God for and be glad about it." (TLB)

That is really my motto now in life. To live life with happiness and meaning, you have to look at the positive side to life and see what God has blessed you with. I know it's so hard to even want to go there when struggling with this painful loss. But if you reflect on your life before this happened, you will see the beauty God has laid out for you.

"The risk of loss is love, and the price of love is grief-
but the pain of grief is only a shadow when compared
with the pain of never risking love."
~Hilary Stanton Zunin~

I wouldn't trade anything I've been through so far, for not losing my daughter means I would have never known her. If I had the choice to have her and she die at 13 years old, or never have her and not know her, I would choose having her and then lose her. She was a gift to me, one I will love and cherish for the rest of my life. Someone I will think about until I take my last breath here on earth.

Tayler changed me forever, and I believe she was the one who "saved my soul." I now depend on God for every day life, never to live without Him again. With God's promise for eternal life, I have hope, peace and gratitude for my Heavenly Father. I could have easily run the other way, living a life of anger, depression and avoiding God. Unfortunately for me, I had to lose my daughter before I sought out God. But, now I choose happiness, and taking a hold onto life again, trying everyday to become the woman

God created me to be. I'm still here for a reason, and I want to see what's in store for me.

GOD KISS

June 16, 2010- I had all of Tayler's friends over for a sleepover, for a summer celebration! Mallory K. was one of Tayler's dearest friends and had gone off into Tayler's room and closet when the other girls were watching a scary movie in the game room. She sat down on the floor of Tayler's closet and started to think about her. She said all of a sudden a very large Orb was right in front of her!!! She was stunned and couldn't take her eyes off of it!! Then right before her eyes, the orb changed into a silhouette shape of Tayler! She said she felt complete warmth all around her. The silhouette then changed back to an Orb and zipped around her. She tried to find it, looking all around her but it was gone! She called me into the closet and told me what just had happened!! There has been so many ways my daughter has communicated to her friends, my friends, and my husband, to let me know she is with us all the time! I love that! I can't wait until Tayler comes to me!

I love this quote, "Often when we lose hope and think it's the end, GOD smiles and says "Relax sweetheart it's just a bend, <u>not</u> the end!" How many days and nights have I lived from the beginning to now, feeling just that way? But I find so much comfort knowing I am not alone in this journey, and will prevail. I have such hope in God's promises that I can wake up each morning with a renewed spirit, ready to take on the new day.

When you see and realize God has been along your side your entire life, you will not ever feel alone again. "Things do happen for a reason," and being a mother who has lost her daughter to still believe that, is an extraordinary place to be.

> James 1:2-4 - "Consider it all joy, my brothers, when you meet trials of various kinds, for you know that the testing of your faith produces steadfastness. And let steadfastness have it's full effect, that you may be perfect and complete, lacking in nothing." (ESV)

There are so many other connections I see that happened throughout my life that are so incredible, now to see and understand "why" they happened. Trials and tribulations all were there to help me grow as a person, for the better. When something bad happens to us, we wonder "why me?" You think it's the worst thing that could possibly happen to you at the time, not knowing what the reason for it was. Whether it's a relationship gone wrong, a loss of a job, financial issues, whatever it may be, just know it happened for a reason, a good reason.

I see how my trials and tribulations helped build my character and perseverance. This definitely was something I needed to support the destiny God has planned for me. I now understand why I was so strong and independent before I knew God. I learned from each trial that happened to me and went forward with strength and confidence, changing and growing from it.

When I was working and had lost my job, my husband happened to close some deals where I didn't have to go back to work full time (He's a Commercial Real Estate Broker). From that point, I got pregnant with my baby girl, and from then on was a stay at home mom. My dreams were coming true. I could be home with both of my kids and do the "mom" thing. I love it! It never once crossed my mind that God was in the midst of my life. Charlie's success, me a stay at home mom now, moving to Westlake, finding this fabulous church home which happened to have this 30 foot in diameter circle in the front of the church.

Now I know my husband's success had to do with God opening the doors for him to succeed, so I could stay at home with my two children, enjoy them full time, move to our dream home, and find our church. When the new sanctuary was built 12 years ago, we were not members then, John our pastor had said, "I would love one day to have a fountain out front". At that time the very large Christmas tree was put there each year until our fountain went up.

2 Corinthians 3:5 - "We don't have the right to
claim that we have done anything on our own. God
gives us what it takes to do all that we do." (CEV)

I believe God knew my future, so He blessed me with so much, a beautiful husband, beautiful children, amazing family and friends, and an incredible Church. He is a loving God and loves me more than I deserve, and He surrounded me with all of this so I could survive this very difficult time in my life. I was so fortunate to spend everyday with my daughter and son instead of having to work. I cherish those moments now, so much and will forever keep them close to my heart.

Being obedient to God daily can be a challenge, the surrendering of our free will to Jesus Christ. But not to me now. It's my deep desire to surrender myself, to live with Christ as the priority in my life. That's what it means to truly "walk the walk" and live according to who God created you to be. The blessing is a changed life and comes through surrender. This will be a journey I will travel for the rest of my life. I want to seek out my purpose, which I know will bring me true joy and peace.

In "Jesus Calling" a daily devotional by Sarah Young, I loved what I read one day. It said "worry is a form of unbelief. God will either take care of the problem or show us how to handle it." (An edited version of Luke 12:22-

31and John 16:33). That statement alone should give us all peace and take away the stress and anxiousness we feel about the unknown. Everything works out for the best if you "give it to God". I have hope and strength, which is God's gift to me through the Holy Spirit, and that get's me up every morning, ready for another day.

"Troubles has a way of pushing us beyond
ourselves where we search out God who is
waiting for us. It causes us to pray and need
Him like nothing else. And it is in prayer that
we find shelter from the storms of life."
~Unknown Author~

"My Daughter Tayler"

"Her life was so special, she was beautiful and kind,
full of life and happiness, I thanked God she was mine.

She was thoughtful and loyal, she touched so many lives,
her gorgeous red hair, and her loving blue eyes.

She was a "mommy's girl", always kissing and hugging me,
my mini-me, my shadow, forever wanting to be with me.

She was an "angel" here on earth, so humble to the core,
worried about others, a great friend and so much more.

I was here for her, my family and life complete,
I couldn't ask for anything more, she was so amazing and sweet.

Out of the blue, she didn't feel well, with strength she went on,
but in pain I could tell her struggle was on.

We hoped and we prayed, asking God to save her,
we stayed by her side, not ever wanting to leave her.

But God knew different, taking her to the heavens above,
no more pain and suffering, for the one that I love.

With this hole in my heart, how does a parent go on?
with the family I have, a husband and a son.

My life has changed forever feeling sadness everyday,
I ask God for his strength and grace when I talk to Him and pray.

I know she's in heaven, one day we all will be,
she is perfect in His eyes, complete and pain free.

My life on earth is missing, my daughter who I adored,
she was so very special, she's in the presence of the Lord.

One day when my time has come and I'm taking my last breath,
my darling daughter Tayler, will guide me to my final rest.

She will lead me to the heavens with a smile upon her face,
so happy we're back together, and in all of God's grace."

I love you Tayler, you were my life, my love, my
forever more.

I love you,
Mom

Chapter 11

"Everyone has his own specific vocation or mission in life…therein he cannot be replaced, nor can his life be repeated. Thus, everyone's task is as unique as his specific opportunity to implement it."
~Viktor Frankl~

What is my purpose Lord? I try to see and understand why this happened to me and my family? Through these past 3 years, I can see so much beauty that has come out of this tragedy. I can see changed lives from my own family, to my friends, and my daughter's friends. I see a deeper faith in a lot of my girlfriends now, and more appreciation for life and family. Like I said before "I don't sweat the small stuff" anymore. Nothing is worth getting angry over, wasting my energy when life is so short. My husband and I chose to go through this journey together, drawing us so much closer along the way. A lot of marriages fail during this process, for the grief is so strong it destroys what foundation the marriage had before. I am a different woman than I was before this, and I am thankful for that alone.

> Acts 20:24- "But I do not account my life of any value nor as precious to myself, if only I may finish my course and the ministry that I received from the Lord Jesus, to testify to the gospel of the Grace of God." (ESV)

Boy, has God given me so much Grace! Another very inspiring and uplifting devotional from "Jesus Calling" I read on March 26th stated: "I have promised many blessings to those who wait on Me: renewed strength, living above one's circumstances, resurgence of hope, awareness of My continual Presence! (Isaiah 40:31) That is exactly what has happened to me! That is not luck or a coincidence. That is God's word working for me. I didn't want to live. I thought my life was over without hope, and didn't think I could make it one more day. I felt so weak and beaten down when this happened to us, I never felt I would be happy ever again.

GOD KISS

July 8, 2010 Tayler's friend Mika was visiting her grandparents in Hawaii when she had her first visitation dream with Tayler. She said she and three other of Tayler's girlfriends were in a backyard when Tayler started to walk towards them. Mika said Tayler was glowing bright and skipped by them and waved. Tayler then started to go up these transparent stairs up to the sky. Before Tayler stepped up to the first step, Mika grabbed her and said "Tayler! Please don't go! I'm so sorry I didn't hang out with you as much! I'm sorry and I miss you so bad!" They were all trying to hold Tayler back from leaving. Then Mika said, "Let's go with her, its not often we get to see her!" So they walked up the stairs with her straight up to heaven! Mika saw clouds and a huge golden gate and it was opened. Tayler was gone. Mika said she remembers Tayler having her hair in a ½ pony tail with hot pink ribbons, she had on her hot pink converse tennis shoes, denim shorts, white shirt with pink sleeves and hot pink hoop earrings! That's my girl!

It was 3 years April 21st, 2012 and I still feel sadness knowing I won't be with her for many years to come. One of my very dear friends Beth said to me, "Ginger, you are going to be here for a long time for God will use you for His Glory"! I don't know how to feel about that statement right now, for missing Tayler is still so fresh on my mind. The thought of staying here until I'm in my 80's-90 doesn't sound very appealing to me at this time in my journey. But, like everything else I've learned, it's not my choice and it never was. I will put the years without Tayler in perspective of eternity with her, and that makes the time waiting to be with her once again, bearable and even brief.

How does one know or figure out what their calling is? God created us all with our own special gifts, and looking at yourself close enough will help you see what those gifts are. "Showing up" and pitching in would make a difference, getting involved, serving Christ.

The number one thing I know is important for the rest of my journey is to glorify God in everything I do. I know my strengths are talking and listening to others in need. I know I am here now to witness to others who have been down this same path as I, for only those who experienced this can truly understand the magnitude of pain and suffering we endure. I truly believe it is called upon me to tell my story to the world. The blessings God has given me, the God kisses he has revealed to me, my beautiful family, my friends, all are part of my testimony to share with others, to help bring others to Christ.

How else will God use me? I still am patiently waiting to see what "doors open" for me. I pray daily "use me God, show me the way". I know what my strengths are, so it's a matter of time before I see what He has in mind for me. God gave me this strength to "serve Him, not for status" so it's up to me to do just that.

I am very fortunate I don't have to work anymore, so I have plenty of time to volunteer whenever and wherever I am needed. Of course, the need is so strong for so many people and issues, I have to be selective to where my strengths can really be used. I still am not 100% better, but well on my way, and helping others really does help you take the focus off of yourself and onto others. It's just that I have to be "thoughtful" of my own feelings at times and be gentle to myself, for some days are still hard to want to be "perky and positive", so only in God's timing, perfect timing.

> 2 Corinthians 1:4- "He comes alongside us when we go through hard times, and before you know it, he brings us alongside someone else who is going through hard times so that we can be there for that person just as God was there for us." (The Message)

This is so true and has happened time after time for me. God is so merciful and loving, He sent so many beautiful people through my door to help in any way they could. They may not stay long, but are there for the moment, day, week or a lifetime, depending on their significance. The two most important commandments are "Love your God with all of your heart, soul, and mind" and "Love your neighbor as yourself." When you think about this incredible world we live in, and all that God has created, and done for you alone, loving God and being thankful everyday is so vital.

When we worship God we focus our heart on God, which puts everything else into proper perspective. Serving others is so important, and it's another way of showing your love and commitment to God. When God becomes your priority, the lesser you become of your old self, and the more you will become who God created you to be.

GOD KISS

July 2010, Lindsay's first visitation dream had Lauren E and Jess B. in it. They met Tayler in the cafeteria after school. They all talked to Tayler, filling her in with their lives. Tayler gave them some gifts and they all felt like she had never left or was gone. None of them were sad at all. As Tayler was about to leave Lindsay said "goodbye Tayler, I love you and I hope to see you again." Then Tayler smiled and said "I love you too!" Tayler had on a blue top that matched the color of her eyes and a pink bow in her hair.

The vivid description of what was said and what Tayler wore, the interaction each of these dreams shows between my daughter and who she is with, are incredible to me and beyond real. This shows the difference between a normal dream and one from God. No matter how much time has passed, the clarity and description remains the same. Normal dream details are usually forgotten very quickly, remembering a few details right when you wake up from that dream.

I am in a Facebook group called "Broken But Not Shattered" and it is women just like me. We share our stories, share our pictures, and comfort each other on a daily basis. I now have met two of these women who happened to live fairly close to me. We met for lunch and before we left, we hugged and felt God gave us each other for life! What amazing connection to have with anyone, little less someone you just met. God's mercies and love was given to us through this tragedy. This is how to heal through serving God in a profound way as this, "Loving Thy Neighbor As Thyself."

I have now been in numerous situations as these, meeting with women going through this same thing. A few are further along then myself and have helped me. That is "paying forward", helping those in recent situations. These women are now very dear to me and we have such a deep bond together. Seeing the person who is ahead of me in this journey, and to see the "light" all around them, the joy in their eyes again, brings me such peace and hope that one day I will be that person too. All the way to my core, in the deepest part of my soul, true joy and love for life once again is where I want to be.

Matthew 5:16- "In the same way, let your light shine
before others, so that they may see your good works,
and give glory to your Father who is in heaven." (ESV)

If we can remember that life is a gift from God, we will be on our way to healing. As long as we live, we have a reason to serve. How we choose to serve it is totally up to us. Like I said before, we can be "bitter or get better", taking one step at a time toward our purpose while still being here. You can choose to live in total darkness, not seeing all of God's blessing in your life, or choose to go forward with your spiritual eyes and ears open, seeing and hearing all of the gifts and beauty around you. This is the path I choose, for I loved life before Tayler's death, and I will live life again with purpose and joy in my heart. I pray to become as "Christ-like" as possible, to see through Christ's eyes and to have faith as a child would. Trusting, loving, and devoting my life to God.

Since this is a "journey" for me, I have to wait patiently to see how to move forward. I continue with my involvement with church, bible studies, and friends in need, but what is "the big picture" for me?

Maybe it's exactly what I am already doing? God gave me these gifts, which I am using, ready and able when needed. Does it have to be any one thing? Probably not, but pursuing what possibilities are available to you, using your strengths that are God's gifts to you, going forward with life, and eager to be that person you were created to be.

GOD KISS

July 2010- Charlie was at the cemetery putting fresh flowers out for Tayler. He does this every Sunday for her. At the exact moment he was kneeling down and placing flowers in the vase on Tayler's marker, a balloon blew up in front of him, between her marker and himself. He picked it up and it read "Happy Fathers Day". He said he didn't think much about it so stuffed it in the bottom of a trash bag. He put more trash on top of the balloon and walked about 20 yards around the corner and pushed the bag down against some shrubs so it wouldn't blow away. He walked back around to Tayler's marker and squatted back down to finish cleaning it. Within a few minutes, the same balloon came out of the bag and blew up in front of him in the exact spot as before, between her marker and himself!! I would say that is a very strong sign Tayler is with him! Charlie tells me this later in the week and while I'm driving my car to meet friends for lunch, I say to Tayler, "really? Can you please send mommy a sign? Daddy has had some amazing things happen for him, so please?" I go to P.F. Changs for lunch with my sorority sisters and at the end of the meal we all reach in for a fortune cookie. There are about 20 to choose from, so we all grab one and mine says "Daughter"! On the back it reads "You will soon emerge victoriously from the maze you've been traveling in!" I am so happy!

Thank you Tayler for this! I still have that fortune in my journal and will keep it forever!

I told Betsy the other day that today if God gave me the choice to have my daughter back without my soul and faith, or to have God #1 in my life without my daughter, I would choose God now first. With God, I have eternal life with Him and all those I love who've gone before me. Without God, I would have Tayler for only a short while, then death without eternal life. Not a real tough decision to make, but it took me a long time to come to this conclusion.

Finally realizing your purpose will help with acceptance. I don't ask "why" anymore, I just ask God, "show me the way and how I can serve you". That alone fills me up with such joy, I accept the direction He's sending me. This is a journey, one that I will follow the rest of my life. There is not a "quick fix" to get there. Time, patience, and trust knowing God will direct my path. The choices are yours, how and which way you travel. With or without God will make all the difference in your life and in your healing. I've lived both ways now, and I choose God as my focus, as my Lord and Savior. Now I have an incredible, and joyous reason to live.

GOD KISS

August 5, 2010- Laraine is a good friend of mine and called me one day crying telling me she had a visitation dream with Tayler! She said she and her daughter Danielle were driving back from a long trip stopping at a road stop along the way. As she was pulling up to another car she saw it was Tayler and I!! She said Tayler was in the back seat and looked beautiful! She said Tayler was smiling and very happy to see them. (She said Tayler looked to be now 15 years old!) Laraine said she reached out to touch Tayler thinking "I won't feel her or she'll vanish because she knew she had passed and was now a spirit." Laraine reached out to touch Tayler and she was real!!! That startled Laraine so she immediately woke up! Laraine was very emotional describing this to me for is was all very real!!

As I stated in Chapter 9 regarding "Tayler's Water Wells for Africa, we have now gone to Ghana, Africa in January of 2013. With one of our pastors and a group of church members, we all went there not knowing what to find or expect. The first day we arrived, we went to see one of the wells. Actually seeing the well and some of the people it served was incredible. But the most emotional part of the whole thing was seeing the plaque engraved with "Donated by Tayler Family, White's Chapel United

Methodist Church, Southlake, Texas"!!! I started to cry and said to the villagers, "That is my daughter, Tayler is my daughter"! I had no idea that my precious daughter's name would be known to all those whom this "well" would serve! That alone made my trip!

Each day from then on we split up into three teams so we could administer medicines to the small villages that were so destitute and poor. Our men helped the local men build two pavilions that will serve as a school or church. On the last day we dedicated and blessed each well, celebrating with them at that time! One of the Ghanaian pastors told me, "Your daughter gave her life to give my people life. Every time we drink from this well, we will think about Tayler"! That statement was so overwhelming and emotional to me, I saw the "beauty out of the ashes", the good that came out of our loss.

Charlie and I were so excited to go there and witness this incredible gift and experience the people and their lives. We fell in love with the Ghanaian people and know this will be a lifelong mission for us. I truly believe this is a huge part of God's plan for our lives. Never in my life did I think I would EVER be involved with something like this!! Never in my life did I EVER think my daughter's legacy would live on through people across the world!! I find my life now so much more purposeful and meaningful than before. My life is so much more enriched, my priorities have changed, and my heart and soul have changed.

"Sometimes in tragedy we find our life's purpose-the
eye shed's a tear to find its focus."
~Robert Brault~

Chapter 12

"I still miss those I loved who are no longer with me
but I find I am grateful for having loved them.
The gratitude has finally conquered the loss."
~Rita Mae Brown~

Sitting out on my back patio, sipping on some French vanilla cappuccino coffee, I read my "One Year Bible". I love the beauty all around me, enjoying the morning breeze, and the birds singing. I feel such peace in my life, knowing God is all around. Both inside and out of me, I feel His presence just wrapping His arms around me, letting me know "I am good."

This journey has been a long and tedious one, continuing, but with hope and joy and a different appreciation for life. There is not a day that goes by without thinking of Tayler, missing her, and cherishing all of the memories with her. One of the phases of grief is "acceptance" and now I can say, I have accepted her death. I give her to God completely, knowing she is in perfect hands, and having an incredible life. What made acceptance so much easier, was not thinking of Tayler in the past, but finally realizing Tayler will be in my future! Hallelujah, praise the Lord!

2 Corinthians 4:16-18 –"So we do not lose heart. Though our outer self is wasting away our inner self is being renewed day by day. For this light momentary affliction is preparing us an eternal weight of glory beyond all comparison, as we look not to the things that are seen but to things that are unseen. For the things that are seen are transient, but the things that are unseen are eternal." (ESV)

I never thought I would want to live at all without my daughter. She had so much life ahead of her, which I was involved in every part, and that's what I miss. This earthly life is all I know, and what I think she is missing is the hard part. What I know about love, family, having a child of your own, dating, marriage, I know Tayler would have loved and cherished all she experienced . She was so focused and conscientious about life, she would have loved it all. Yes, I know I am being selfish wanting her back with me, but I'm her mom, and loved her more than life itself. My strong faith is what gets me by, day after day, and I know she is where we all want to be. I am relieved to know I will never have to leave her now and thankful I know where she is, with all of my family who has gone before me.

My husband and son are so precious in my life, each of us still taking one day at a time. My son is still young, finishing school, and has a lot of life yet to live. I pray everyday that he becomes the man Christ created him to be. There are so many things yet he has to experience, I look forward being there for him and with him through each phase of his life. Maybe a granddaughter one day, with strawberry blonde hair and blue eyes ☺? Who knows what God has planned for my son? Whatever that may be, I will love and cherish my son throughout his journey.

Living the life of a Christian doesn't guarantee a perfect life. Everyone will suffer and have struggles. I love the quote, "Without a mess there would be no message, without a test there would be no testimony." That is so true so to live a life of happiness, we must all do our best and let God do the rest! I truly don't know how anyone lives on without the Lord in their life. With eternal promises of pure joy, no more pain and suffering, why would anyone choose not to? Pride, ego, stubbornness are all traits of sin that will wall up the truth. It's Satan doing his best work, keeping those cynical thoughts in your mind at all times. I did the same thing. When I was younger and had accepted Christ as my savior, my heart was open and wanting. As I aged even having this deep belief within my soul, I became cynical and doubtful, as a lot of people do. I depended on this world to make me happy and complete, getting further away from God.

GOD KISS

October 1, 2010, Enoch Sng (Tayler's friend) had a dream that he was at a school function and as he was walking around he saw Tayler. He said she looked like she was 15, like she would've been. They talked about things going on at school and Tayler said "everything is going great." He said she was so happy to see everyone and that she missed everyone. Enoch felt she had just moved away and that he would always get to see her again. When he woke up he realized this was a dream, but it was very real.

All I know is that God has filled up the hole in my heart and I do want to live out my days through Him, glorifying Him, and serving Him. I am a completely different woman today, and for the best. I will never leave or forsake God again. But to do that, I have to trust Him and live each day to the fullest. It may sound exhausting, but it's not. Just take one day at a time, not wasting any energy on worrying, being angry, stressing out about anything. I have such inner peace now in my life, I can manage this most of the time.

Mark 3:36- "What good is it for someone to gain
the whole world, yet forfeit their soul?" (NIV)

I now see so many people around me going after things that are so trivial. It's been going on for years, and centuries to achieve stuff, live the "high life", to keep up with the Joneses, but that verse states it perfectly. What's the point if you forfeit your soul? We only chase those things, those reputations because we are lacking something else inside. Have you ever wondered why none of this fills you up? Constantly searching for something that will never matter in the end? Look around you, your loved ones who just want your time. Love is what life is all about. If you are blessed like I have been, having a wonderful husband and blessed with children, you are half way there! Take the time to "smell the roses" and enjoy the life God has given you. I had to lose my precious daughter before I realized what and how I was living. Even though my family was my life, I left out God, who should be first and foremost.

The "high" I feel from having God in my life now far outweigh anything else I have ever had or experienced. Getting to know Christ personally fills me up and makes me feel whole again. Better than a best friend. Sharing your problems with Him, finding comfort in His presence, knowing He will never disappoint you or betray you, total trust.

I can also calmly go through my day with a lot of peace, trusting whatever God has planned for me. It doesn't mean you have to be working constantly, for works alone doesn't mean anything either. Some days, I might enjoy the beauty of my backyard, other days I may be consoling someone from a loss. Going to my bible studies, the gym, or having lunch with a friend, all of this is healing to my soul. I like so many others used to be in such a hurry to finish things, to get where I was going, always frantic, stressed and on edge, never enough time in the day. I rarely had any peace or quiet to just be. But then God wasn't a priority in my life and that is key. Loving yourself enough to make time, to pray and be thankful everyday for God, your life and family. Trusting God enough to "give Him your worries or problems" is such a huge weight off of my shoulders. That's what gives me true peace.

I love to read and learn anything about my faith and God. I came across this saying and it is so true: "When God solves your problems you have faith in His abilities. When God doesn't solve your problems, He has faith in your abilities!" We are not puppets and He is not a puppet master, but we are people with brains who have choices to make. Even though we will make choices that are not God's way, He will allow us to make them, probably stumbling, with all kinds of road blocks. We are to live and learn, seeing our mistakes along the way so we turn back in the right direction, in God's direction for us.

> Romans 14:11- it is written: "As surely as I live,
> says the Lord, every knee will bow before me;
> every tongue will acknowledge God." (NIV)

Traveling though this journey, having God now in my life has helped me endure and live through this great suffering. Suffering is God's way for us to grow spiritually. But suffering alone won't do the job. Depending on how you respond to the suffering will determine if the pain will take you deeper in your walk with God. To seek trust in God more fully will happen with having this kind of faith. God's blessing is not that he gives us what we want, but when we are in these painful places, he gives us himself.

Finding joy in suffering, something good that comes out of it, is discovering that your faith is genuine, real. Experiencing all I have so far has only confirmed what I never knew before. God is for real, and therefore, eternal life and heaven is for real for all who believe! So, biblical hope is much more than wishful thinking. Hebrews 11:1 says that "Faith is being sure of what we hope for and certain of what we do not see." (NIV) Biblical hope is something we haven't yet experienced, but there is not doubt that it will happen.

I have on my bulletin board Romans 8:28- "And we know that God causes all things to work together for the good for those who love God, to those who are called according to His purpose." I struggled with that bible verse for a very long time, for to me NOTHING was worth losing my daughter to. NOTHING would be better than my daughter ever was to me. But today, I will say, the ultimate good that came out of this nightmare, is my relationship with God. Having Him in my life gives me the pure joy of being with my baby forever. Having God in my life now, gives me His promises of a perfect life with Him and Tayler for all eternity!

GOD KISS

December 22, 2010- I had lunch with my sister Kathy and she told me about what happened with my mom's phone. (My Mom passed away September 7th, 2010). This was the week before Christmas and my sister was in her kitchen. Kathy was the executor of my mom's estate, so therefore, took care of all of the financial accounts, business accounts, paying bills, etc. My sister had cancelled her cell phone account in September. There was no longer an account, it was turned off, and placed in the nightstand in my sister's bedroom. Now my mom had an alarm set on her phone to remind her of any bridge games she had coming up. It was some kind of music that was loud enough she could hear to get her up and on her way. Ok, so here it is the week before Christmas and out of the blue, this alarm goes off, loud and clear! My sister stops, frozen, shocked, and wanders into her bedroom toward the music. She opens the drawer and there the alarm on my mom's phone is sounding off!!! This phone has had no service now for over 3 months now, hasn't even been charged up for that length of time too! I told Kathy, "No surprise, Mom is trying to let you know she is with you during this holiday!" My sister has been cynical before and didn't know what to think about this! I know, I've been there through so many signs, this one's for my sister from my mom!

I love this quote, "A little faith will bring your soul to heaven, but a lot of faith will bring heaven to your soul." (Dwight L. Moody) That is so true. I find my daily life now to have and feel so much more peace than before. I lost my mom in 2010, and seeing her take her last breath, holding her hand and kissing her goodbye, brought me to a place I wouldn't have felt or experienced before losing Tayler. I know 100% she is now with God and all of my loved ones who have passed on before her. She is in perfect health and loving her new phase of life with her mother, sister, husband and Tayler.

Philippians 1:21- "For to me to live is
Christ, and to die is gain." (NIV)

I find it quite amazing how much more confident I am in who I am now. I thought I was before, but that was "a false confidence". I don't seek anything of little value, of little meaning, of little purpose any more. I have a much higher standard of living. Not in the sense of financial means, but in depth and love. Joy is more prevalent in my life. In Matthew 5:5- "You're blessed when you're content with just who your are, no more no less. That's the moment you find yourselves proud owners of everything that can't be bought." (The Message)

Who would have thought after going to college for my "big career", to be that strong, independent woman who strived for "the nice things in life" to find happiness would be saying this? I am not saying to have or want nice things is a bad thing, it's just putting it in the correct level of priority in your life. Remember, God wants us all to prosper in life, through loving Him, helping others and helping ourselves. That is true prosperity. If we are blessed with financial success then it is our responsibility to use it not only for ourselves and family, but to help others. In Matthew 6:24, "No one can serve two masters. Either you will hate the one and love the other, or you will be directed to the one and despise the other. You cannot serve both God and money." (NIV)

GOD KISS

February 13, 2011- Charlie and I went to San Francisco for the week. Betsy, our pastor told us "take Tayler with you." Of course, the trainee checking us in at our hotel's name was Taylor, the street sign name crossing the street our hotel was on was Taylor street, and when sightseeing we saw "Taylor" painted on a sign for a child's bedroom. By the end of the week, Tayler came to her dad in a visitation dream. Charlie said we were on a trolley car and when it came to a stop at the light, Tayler walked around the corner. She had a bright pink coat on, stud earrings on and her hair was pulled back in a bun. He got out of the trolley car and they walked toward each other and began to hug each other. Charlie said when they pulled away, he stared at every inch of her face. Her skin was beautiful and clear, very natural and pretty. She had a solemn look on her face and she said with a very clear voice, "Dad, I am right here." Not smiling, but trying to let him realize in the tone of her voice, "Don't you understand I am with you all of the time". He said they hugged again and then she turned away, walking a dog that looked just like our collie "Prince", but his coloring was different. A week and a half later, our "Prince" died. The day after his death, I went on Facebook to post this and went through the 2,000 pictures I have to find a picture of him to post. I stated what happened and posted his picture on my personal page, went to my "wall" and instead of his picture and this statement was 2 pictures of Tayler and her marker at the cemetery. It said I had posted that 17 seconds ago. I immediately called my son to see if he had been on my Facebook page and he said no. So I re-posted Prince's picture and status, and when I went back to my wall to see if it was there, Tayler's pictures were gone and Prince's was there! I truly believe Tayler was letting me know Prince is with her!

Of course I am thrilled to hear of each and every one of these dreams, visions, signs, whatever it may be, but I am also sad Tayler hasn't come to me yet. I did read in one of the "life after death" books that "until you can live life without depending on your loved one for "living", they won't come to you. I know Tayler wants me to live my life with happiness and joy, not dwelling on her absence, and I'm trying really hard, and I'm getting there. I know in God's timing, she will come to me. Charlie told me, "When she does come to you, you will be sad and cry all over because she will leave again." But I believe her coming will help me so much more, seeing for myself, my baby, hearing her voice, hugging her and holding her one more time. I can't wait for that day.

"We are not human beings on this earth
experiencing spiritual life…we are spiritual
beings on this earth experiencing human life."
~Dr. Wayne W. Dyer~

God created this beautiful earth, with all of these beautiful people who have souls. We were all created in His image and to seek and want God in our lives. What happens along the way to that, is human living. There is so much we don't know or understand. Our very small brains can't even begin to "understand" God and how this all works. But the one thing I know through my journey, I have no doubt that this life here on earth is so short, and just the beginning to a life of pure beauty, happiness, and love that will go way beyond anything I have experienced here on this earth. We will all have eternal life, we just have to decide where we will spend it. That alone is a serious and scary realization for those who have no clue.

What I do know for sure now, this is my training ground, to become the woman I was created to be, and I plan on achieving everything God has in store for me. That's how I "live around this hole". The one and only way, making God the #1 priority in my life, living like my daughter would want me to, completing my journey according to his plan, glorifying Him always, and truly living life to the fullest.

I pray that who ever reads my book will see God, seek out God and make Him your life. I can't "save" you for you already have a "Savior". It's up to you to want to make a change, one that will make your life so much better than you can imagine. It's the only way to be completely fulfilled and live truly happy. My life has changed because I did make this choice. I choose life, I choose joy, and I choose God.

Chapter 13

"The term for these "Kisses" are called
"Epiphanies", which literally mean "the
manifestations of God". It is said that epiphanies
bring light and remind us that God is with us."
~Susan Duke~

I believe in Angels and guardian Angels. I've always believed
in the spiritual world and so wasn't so surprised when these
"spiritual orbs" started to show up in my pictures. I read
so much from the beginning, trying to get answers, or just
understand "why". Of course, there was not one book that
could give me what I wanted, so I read everything from
near death experiences, the loss of other children, the after
life, Angels, and then eventually the Bible. I also stated
in Chapter 9 my dream with the orb and my daughter's
initials coming out of it, and then in Chapter 10, Tayler's
friend Mallory saw an orb form change shapes into Tayler's
silhouette, then disappear right in front of her own eyes as
she sat wide awake! These two events tie in together this

chapter of orbs in these pictures and why I know they are spiritual beings, and really feel they are my daughter in all of these pictures you are about to see. I have a lot of family members already in heaven so I'm sure they are with her also.

I went back throughout our pictures over the past 13 years and until Tayler got sick was there not one orb! These next few pictures were taken one month before she was diagnosed with Leukemia. In picture #1 you will see Tayler in the bathroom and there are two small orbs around her. On the right of the doorframe, below the large stripe you will see a large orb.

Picture #1

One of the first books I read about orbs was from someone who had lost their loved one. They said "when you are sad and depressed, call out to who has passed on and start to take pictures." I thought, "what the heck?" I was having a tough day and was in my bedroom alone watching T.V. So I got my digital camera and started to talk to my daughter Tayler. I told her that I was taking a shower and for her to come with me. I walked into my closet, still talking to her, got my pajamas and continued into the shower. Before I left my closet I turned off the light so there would not be any dust, a flash or a reflection in the picture. I took multiple pictures not having any clue what I was aiming at and then continued to the shower. (I didn't want to have any doubt of what I would see, if anything).

From there, I went into my shower and continued to talk to Tayler. Once I was through, I dried off and took more pictures inside the shower, again with the lights off. As I went back into my bedroom, I continued to take pictures and talk to Tayler some more. I immediately downloaded the pictures on my computer and this is what I saw.

Picture #2

If you notice the "white" circle or orb to the left of my light in my closet on the ceiling. (picture #2) There are also two small orbs also in this picture. The next picture will be in my shower and you will see the "orb" in the corner up at the top of the shower. (picture #3)

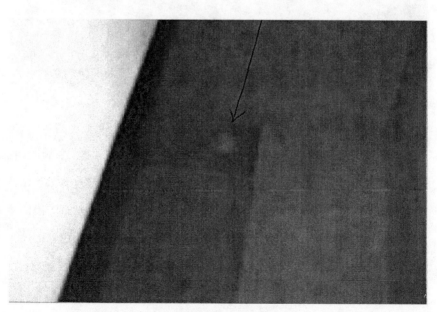

Picture #3

When I entered my bedroom I once again took more pictures and this is what I saw. (picture #4) The very large and bright orb is to the left of the ceiling fan. I was astonished and very excited to know that possibly Tayler or a loved one was with me.

Picture #4

These pictures were taken September 9, 2009, which was early on during my journey. When I told my husband what I witnessed, he took my camera and turned off all of the lights in the house and walked all around including upstairs. As he was coming down the back stairs, he turned to take a picture and this is what he saw. (picture #5)

Picture #5

Can you see the large orb right above the mirror at the top of the picture? Tayler was probably following her Dad and thinking, "what are you doing Dad"?

The next night I called Aleda and Nyse over and Nyse said, "Mr. Charlie, let's go up to Tayler's room and try it"! So they went upstairs to her room and went into total darkness. (picture #6) While Nyse took pictures, Charlie picked up Tayler's piggy and said, "Tayler I have

Picture #6

your piggy!" Can you see the bright orb under her piggy? The room is pitch black and Charlie has his eyes closed. This is another random shot and the orb is right above the purple curtain. (picture #7)

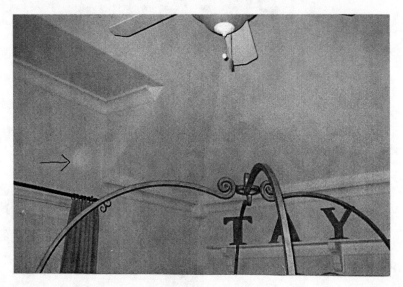

Picture #7

The next holiday was Halloween 2009. My daughter loved Halloween and we used to really go over-board with the decorations. Because it was so soon after her passing, (only 6 months), we decided to do something small for her friends, a party and sleepover. Charlie and I decorated the upstairs game room. Before the girls showed up I took a picture of the decorated area and this is what was there. We have spiders of all sizes hanging from the ceiling and cobwebs all over the furniture. To the left of the Mummy you can see the bottom of a very large orb. (picture #8)

Picture #8

Here's a picture of my son Chase. (Picture #9 Notice the orb to the left of Chase's forehead.

Picture #9

It seems that finding these orbs are usually during Holidays of some sort. Whether it's birthday parties for Tayler, Halloween, or Christmas celebrations, these orbs show up. Not in any other pictures, but ones of important gatherings.

GOD KISS

A young man named Jack D. was a peer of Tayler's but I never heard her talk about him. He wrote me to tell me even though he didn't know her, he was having a quiet moment with God and praying and he describes what he saw was nothing of this world. He said "my eyes were open and the next thing I see is a cemetery and Tayler was dancing in the most beautiful way. She was gracefully twirling around, just pure joy and passion. It was so completely amazing watching her. He said, I know a cemetery has a negative connotation for most people, but this vision was the complete opposite. This was filled with so much joy and happiness and the presence of God. Tayler gave me the message that she is extremely happy, beyond what we can ever imagine while here on earth. He said that she was older, like the age she would be if still here (15 yrs. old) , her hair was a lot longer and darker and she was also taller. She was wearing a long white dress. He said she had gotten so close to God that it was her unique and individual self but to such a complete and whole level.

She sent me the vision to show me her completeness of God, complete lack and disappearance of death in her life, to show me she was living a real life with God and Jesus and she was always with us with God, watching over us."

For my son's 21st birthday in January 2010 , I invited all of the girls to come have lunch with us. They all adored Chase, so he was happy to have them. After lunch, we went up to Tayler's room to sit and chat. Nyse started to take pictures and the reflection inside the TV was incredible! The "Star of David" was bright as can be! (picture #10)

Picture #10

Just another God kiss to show He is with me during this journey! You can also see an orb above the left corner of the TV.

The next weekend Nyse had a bunch of girls over for a sleepover. Steve, Nyse's dad who was a cynic and realist (and a lawyer too), took pictures of them that night outside for me. (Picture #11)

Picture #11

The first picture is a picture of them on Nyse's front lawn. These were taken January 17th, 2010. The large orb is to the left of the girls. The next picture notice the orb above the girls heads on the left in picture #12

Picture #12

The next big event we had was for Relay for Life, our "Team Tayler". This took place in April 2010. At first we had a round robin dinner party at three different houses. Once we were at our house for dessert, I took a few pictures. This first one is of the girls on our team (all of Tayler's closest friends) sitting on our front stairway of our house. (picture #13) Notice the orb on Brooklynne's sleeve, the girl with the long brown hair nearest to the flower arrangement. It's small so look closely.

Picture #13

The next picture is of a few friends looking at the scrapbooks I made of Tayler's life. (picture #14) As they were sitting around our coffee table I took this picture. There is a very bright orb to the left upper right hand corner, right above our lamp and one on the right side of the windowpane.

Picture #14

In May 2010, we had our Relay for Life walk and had to create a theme for our tent. I took pictures that evening of our tent. As you can tell, Tayler loved color, rainbows and butterflies, therefore, that's what our theme was. The first picture with the rainbow on the front has a bright orb right above the "A". Small but distinct.

Picture #15

This next picture is another view of our tent. (picture #16)

Picture #16

You will see a small orb above the large butterfly balloon.

"The very presence of an Angel is a communication.
Even when an Angel crosses our path in silence, God
has said to us, "I am here, I am present in your life."
~Tobias Palmer~

That same summer of June 2010, Nyse and Mika came over to spend the night with us. They were on the back stairs when Patches, Tayler's cat, ran up past them. In this photo, Mika turns to catch the cat when an orb took off and the orb was caught in action! You will notice the "streak" of light above Mika's head. (picture #17)

Picture #17

You should be able to tell there is a common thread in all of these pictures. Whenever we get together in memory of Tayler, or just any holiday, orbs appear. I truly believe our loved ones are with us, more than we know. I just wish I would know when, possibly see or feel her, but I know I'm asking too much for now. Maybe in God's time? I hope so.

Angels, guardian angels, loved ones, I believe these orbs are exactly that. I want to believe Tayler is with us during these special moments. This was her "heaven" here on earth, and I believe she spends these times with her loved ones still here when she can.

All of these pictures were taken during different times of the day, with different cameras, by different people. These are signs, "God kisses" from God, to once again give me another day of peace, and joy knowing my baby girl is not far from us.

When my husband Charlie went to Beijing to see the very first finished sculpture of our statue for the fountain we donated to our church, a picture was taken of both my husband and the Chinese sculptor. The statue was first carved out of clay. Here you will see on my husband's jacket a very large orb on it. To the left of the Chinese man there is another very large orb and also to the left of Jesus's foot.

Now my thoughts and beliefs were this were my daughter Tayler, Dado-Charlie's father and other relatives who have passed. Who knows, but I love feeling like they were possibly there loving what was being done, both in memory of my daughter and to glorify God. Look below to picture #18 for these details.

Picture #18

Christmas 2010 have again orbs in various shots. In picture #19 you will see a large bright orb to the left on the wall, and notice our dog Prince is in this picture.

Picture #19

Picture #20 there is a large bright orb floating above the dining table.

Picture #20

The next time I took pictures was the last big hurrah for the girls to come over and hang out, swim and eat before school started that year. This next picture is all of the girls on Tayler's trampoline, and it's about 4:00 pm in the afternoon. To the left of Lindsay (the girl in the pink top) is a very bright orb!! Tayler wouldn't miss her peeps at her own house! She always loved a good party! (picture #21)

Picture #21

Each year on Tayler's birthday we have a get-together with everyone. We took the girls to Hurricane Harbor, dinner, and the cemetery to release balloons, then to the fountain we built in honor of our daughter to see it lit at night. (Picture #22)

Picture #22

To the right side of the statue of Jesus you will see a bright orb. It looks like it could be the moon, but it's not. (picture #22)

Another Christmas goes by (2011) and again the camera is clicking away. These are on Christmas morning before and after we opened presents. Right above Charlie's head is an orb. (picture #23)

Picture #23

The right of Cydney's head is another orb. (picture #24)

Picture #24

The next picture, the orb is quite bright and at the top of the ceiling. (picture #25) They do move around and so you see them in different places. Or, there could be more than one spirit with us?

Picture #25

Picture #26 is in Ghana, Africa, January 2013. We went there with our church for "Tayler's Water Wells for Africa" and to give out medicines to the village people. Notice the very large orb on the nurse's baseball cap!

Picture #26

Just because our loved ones aren't with us and in Heaven I feel they come and go, spending these wonderful times with us, cherishing them with us, seeing that we are hopefully carrying on with life the best possible way we can. Thank you Lord for these wonderful glimpses!

GOD KISSES

Nyse had a visitation dream the night before school started her junior year. She said that she was looking around to see who was in her classroom and next to her and there was Tayler! She was smiling at Nyse and her teeth were perfectly straight! (This is the first time anyone mentioned her teeth without braces.) She said her hair was blonde on top and darker on the bottom (that's my daughter, changing her hair color). She said she wore a pink t-shirt with denim shorts. Nyse said she started to cry and Tayler came up to her and hugged her! Nyse was so happy to know Tayler was with her still at school!

Just to give you an update on "what is my purpose?" I have prayed continually "God use me, open the doors you want me to step into." Well, the bible study women's group I've been going to now for 2 ½ years approached me to be a "servant leader." I was so honored they would feel I was strong and capable enough to join them! I happily agreed to join them, anxious to get the fall season started!

Shortly after that, do you remember the "Mission Committee" I am on at our church? The lead pastor pulled me aside and asked me if I would be interested to work part-time in place of another lady leaving on maternity leave! I wasn't seeking out work at all. I never thought I would ever work a job again, so again I was surprised and honored she would even ask me!

Compassionate Friends, the national grief group I had talked about? I was given an "okay" to contact the national headquarters to start up a chapter at our church. Well, it also is coming true. We will have this chapter to serve our community, as well as the surrounding cities around us. We have a huge need for something like this, for other grief groups don't work for those who have lost a child. God opened up these doors for me to walk through, serving Him, glorifying Him, and living my life through Him! Praise God and thank you for answering my prayers!

Well, my book is complete but my journey is not. I am a "Jesus follower" and until I take my last breath will I serve God by serving my purpose. I am a different woman today, and I thank my Lord, and I give thanks to my precious daughter saving my soul! Without her and this even taking place in my life, I doubt I would cherish my relationship with God and be so thankful to all He has done for me my whole life. Glory be to God and I love you Tayler!

A CLOSING WORD
FROM THE AUTHOR

Thirteen chapters for thirteen beautiful years with Tayler. I will never forget her, but I am changed forever. She is so much who I am now, I thank God everyday for her life and now mine.

I am living happily in Westlake, Texas with my husband of 34 years. We are very involved with our son who is finishing up college. We appreciate every minute we have together, enjoying each aspect life brings us.

My husband and I are very active in our church, seeking out our purpose God has for us. We live our lives now taking one day at a time, giving back for all that God has given us.

From this book, I pray that others who have experienced the loss of their child, that they find peace and hope once again. I pray that they see God throughout my journey, therefore they seek God for their lives. I pray that this book helps us continue our mission for Tayler's Water Wells for Africa and that we can continue to drill wells for those people in need.

If you would like to contact me, you can go to my webpage at www.GingerReynoldsGodKisses.com and there you can go to my blog page and write me your experiences, your comments and see what has been opened up to me as my life continues. If you would like to make a direct donation to Tayler's Water Wells for Africa, you can go to my Church website at www.whiteschapelumc.com and click on Donations, click on the drop down menu and click on Tayler's Water Wells for Africa. I am also Co-leading "The Compassionate Friends chapter in Southlake Texas. This is such an incredible National grief group that helps others who have also lost a child. I feel this is my purpose in life now, to help others deal with their loss. To give them hope and peace, knowing they can live with joy in their lives once again. God is so good and I am blessed! God Bless You!

NOTES

"COMPASSIONATE FRIENDS"
Address: P.O. Box 3696
Oak Brook IL 60522-3696
Website: WWW.COMPASSIONATEFRIENDS.ORG
To find a chapter near you

AUTHORS:
Chapter 9- "There are no coincidences in life. They are actually small miracles where God chooses to remain anonymous." By Patti Miller Dunham in, "I Saw Heaven"- Chapter 12 page 125

Chapter 13- "The term for these "Kisses" are called "Epiphanies", which literally mean "the manifestations of God." It is said that epiphanies bring light and remind us that God is with us." Susan Duke, "Grieving Forward"- page 170

Chapter 10-"Worry is a form of unbelief. God will either take care of the problem or show us how to handle it." By Sarah Young "Jesus Calling"- page 166

Chapter 11- "I have promised many blessings to those who wait on Me: renewed strength, living above one's circumstances, resurgence of hope, awareness of My continual presence!" By Sarah Young "Jesus Calling"- page 89

The back of my book-Marsha Maring, author of "I know The Secret", is her story through the death of her son, divorce and other challenges she experienced. She explains how her path in life has been directed by God but orchestrated by people. A must read for those suffering through life's struggles and needing to find peace and hope once again.

BIBLE VERSES

Psalms 91:15   "When they call on me, I will answer; I will be with them in trouble." (NLT)

Deuteronomy 31:18-   "The Lord himself goes before you and will be with you; He will never leave you nor forsake you. Do not be afraid; do not be discouraged." (NIV)

James 4:14-   "Yet you do not know what tomorrow will bring. What is your life? For you are a mist that appears for a little time and then vanishes." (ESV)

Job 14:5-   "Since his days are determined, the number of his month is with you; and his limits you have set so that he cannot pass." (NASB)

Psalms 116:15-   "Precious in the sight of the Lord is the death of His Godly ones." (NASB)

Mathew 17:20-   "You don't have enough faith", Jesus told them. I tell you the truth, if you have faith even as small as a mustard seed, you could say to this mountain "move from here to there", and it would move." (NLT)

Psalms 6:8- "And I believed the Lord…heard the voice of my weeping." (NASB)

Philippians 3:12-14- "I am not saying that I have this all together, that I have it made. But I am well on my way, reaching out for Christ, who has so wondrously reached out for me. Friends, don't get me wrong: by no means do I count myself an expert in all of this, but I have got my eye on the goal, where God is beckoning us onward to Jesus. I'm off and running, and I'm not turning back!" (MSG)

Daniel 6:10- "We stand tallest and strongest on our knees." (NASB)

Jeremiah 29:11- "For I know the plans I have for you "declares the Lord"; plans to prosper you and not harm you, plans to give you hope and a future." (NIV)

Isaiah 42:10- "Fear not, for I am with you; be not dismayed, for I am your God; I will strengthen you, I will help you, I will uphold you with my righteous right hand." (NIV)

Galatians 2:20- "I have been crucified with Christ. It is no longer I who live, but Christ who lives in me. And the life I now live in the flesh I live by faith in the Son of God, who loved me and gave me himself for me." (ESV)

1 Corinthians 2:9-10- "However, how it is written: "No eye has seen, no ear has heard, no mind has conceived, what God has prepared for those who love Him." (NIV)

Philippians 3:8- "What is more I consider everything a loss compared to the surpassing greatness of knowing Christ Jesus my Lord, for whose sake I have lost all things. I consider them rubbish, that I may gain Christ." (NIV)

Romans 8:28- "And we know that God causes all things to work together for the good for those who love God, to those who are called according to his purpose." (NASB)

Isaiah 40:31- "But those who hope in the Lord will renew their strength. They will soar on wings like eagles; they will run and not grow weary, they will walk and not be faint." (NIV)

John 3:16- "For God so loved the world, that He gave His only Son, that whoever believes in Him should not perish but have eternal life." (ESV)

Philippians 4:8-	"Think about things that are pure and lovely, and dwell on the fine, good things…Think about all you can praise God for and be glad about it." (TLB)
James 1:2-4-	"Consider it all joy, my brothers, when you meet trials of various kinds, for you know that the testing of your faith produces steadfastness. And let steadfastness have it's full effect, that you may be perfect and complete, lacking in nothing." (ESV)
2 Corinthians 3:5-	"We don't have the right to claim that we have done anything on our own. God gives us what it takes to do all that we do." (CEV)
Acts 20:24-	"But I do not account my life of any value nor as precious to myself, if only I may finish my course and the ministry that I received from the Lord Jesus, to testify to the gospel of the Grace of God." (ESV)
2 Corinthians 1:4-	"He comes alongside us when we go through hard times, and before you know it, he brings us alongside someone else who is going through hard times so that we can be there for that person just as God was there for us." (MSG)

Matthew 5:16-	"In the same way, let your light shine before others, so that they may see your good works, and give glory to your Father who is in heaven." (ESV)
2 Corinthians 4:16-18-	"So we do not lose heart. Though our outer self is wasting away, our inner self is being renewed day by day. For this light momentary affliction is preparing us an eternal weight of glory beyond all comparisons, as we look not to the things that are seen but to things that are unseen. For the things that are seen are transient, but the things that are unseen are eternal. (ESV)
Mark 3:36-	"What good is it for someone to gain the whole world, yet forfeit their soul?" (NIV)
Romans 14:11-	"It is written: "As surely as I live, says the Lord, every knee will bow before me; every tongue will acknowledge God." (NIV)
Hebrews 11:1-	"Faith is being sure of what we hope for and certain of what we hope for and certain of what we do not see." (NIV)
Philippians 1:21-	"For to me to live is Christ, and to die is gain." (NIV)
Matthew 5:5-	"You're blessed when you're content with just who you are, no more no less.

That's the moment you find yourselves proud owners of everything that can't be bought." (MSG)

Matthew 6:24-   "No one can serve two masters. Either you will hate the one and love the other, or you will be directed to the one and despise the other. You cannot serve both God and money." (NIV)

BIBLE VERSES BY CHAPTER

INSPIRATIONAL QUOTES

Chapter 1:

"Diseases can be our spiritual flat tires", words by Bernie S. Siegel

Chapter 2:

"Life is like a library owned by the author", words by Harry Emerson Fosdick

Chapter 3:

"Death is nothing else but going home to God", words by Mother Teresa

Chapter 4:

"There is sacredness in tears", words by Washington Irving

Chapter 5:

"The pain of parting is nothing to the joy of meeting again", words by Charles Dickens, Nicholas Nickleby

Chapter 6:

"I suddenly saw that all the time it was not I who had been seeking God", words by Bede Griffiths

Chapter 8:

~"Example is not the main thing in influencing others", words by Albert Schweitzer

Chapter 9:

~"Healing does not mean going back to the way things were before" words by Ram Dass

"~Trials and tribulations build character" words by Unknown Author

Chapter 10:

~"When we embrace the many parts of our experience we discover a magnificent creation" words by Debbie Milam

~"The risk of loss is love, and the price of love is grief", words by Hilary Stanton Zunin

~"Troubles has a way of pushing us beyond ourselves where we search out God", words by Unknown Author

Chapter 11:

~"Everyone has his own specific vocation or mission in life…" words by Viktor Frankl

~"Sometimes in tragedy we find our life's purpose" words by Robert Brault

Chapter 12:

~"I still miss those I loved who are no longer with me but I find I am grateful for having loved them" words by Rita Mae Brown

~"A little faith will bring your soul to heaven, but a lot of faith will bring heaven to your soul" words by Dwight L. Moody

~"We are not human beings on this earth experiencing spiritual life" words by Dr. Wayne W. Dyer

Chapter 13:

~"The term for these "kisses" are called "Epiphanies", which literally mean "the manifestations of God" words by Susan Duke, author of "Grieving Forward". Her website is www.suzieduke.com

~"The very presence of an Angel is a communication" words by Tobias Palmer

SONGS

"The Climb" – written by Jessi Alexander and Jon Mabe in 2009

"Amazing Grace" written by John Newton in 1779

POEMS

Chapter 3:

"A Butterfly" words by Unknown Author

Chapter 6:

"My Life in You" words by Ginger Reynolds

Chapter 10:

"My Daughter Tayler" words by Ginger Reynolds

BOOKS

"I Saw Heaven!" by Patti Miller Dunham- Chapter 9

"Jesus Calling" by Sarah Young – Chapters 10 and
Chapter 11

"Grieving Forward" by Susan Duke- Chapter 13

"I Know The Secret" by Marsha Maring- back cover of
my book

CPSIA information can be obtained at www.ICGtesting.com
Printed in the USA
LVOW08s0152100813

347114LV00003B/6/P